ENDORS

Mike Bensi has created a great resource for any leader, regardless of their experience level, with this book. The Success of Failure provides insight into a number of important professional and personal issues not commonly addressed in other management or leadership books.

- Ted Maple, Ph.D., President and CEO, Early Learning Indiana

The Success of Failure will resonate with managers new and old who face success, failure and conflict. What Mike Bensi does Is demonstrate how you and your team can grow from these experiences.

- Craig P. Anderson, President, Student Connections

The Success of Failure won't only produce better managers, but if its wisdom is consistently applied, it will also make those managers better, more peaceful and effective people.

- David Forsell, President, Keep Indianapolis Beautiful

The Success of Failure puts a human perspective on lessons that apply to the entry-level manager up to the CEO. The book features relatable characters that inspire thoughtful change in both behavior and mindset. It's a must-read for anyone who wants to improve themselves and the people they lead.

- Nick Smarrelli, CEO, GadellNet

The Success of Failure is a journey that never ends. Mike Bensi does a great job portraying the importance of work life balance at any level of leadership.

- Jonathan Desalvo , President, Arcamed

THE SUCCESS OF FAILURE

THE SUCCESS OF FAILURE

A coming-of-age fable about **overcoming failure** despite ourselves

MIKE BENSI

NEW YORK
NASHVILLE • MELBOURNE • VANCOUVER

The Success of Failure

A coming-of-age fable about overcoming failure despite ourselves

Published in New York, New York, by Morgan James Publishing. Morgan James is a trademark of Morgan James, LLC. www.MorganJamesPublishing.com

ISBN 9781683504245 paperback
ISBN 9781683504252 eBook
Library of Congress Control Number: 2017901128

Cover Design by:
Nicholas Bensi

Rachel Lopez
www.r2cdesign.com

Interior Design by:
Chris Treccani
www.3dogdesign.net

DEDICATION

To my wife, Quinn
and my children Aden, Will, and Jacob
I continue to learn so much from your love and support

CONTENTS

PREFACE

The topic of leadership development in today's workforce makes many CEOs and top leaders nervous. Organizations are either unsure of what new generations need in the workforce or unwilling to change past practices to accommodate the need for a people-centered culture. As younger generations continue to grow in number within the workforce, they are increasingly taking on new leadership and management roles. Organizations are unable to support the conversation needed to guide new generations into leadership and management roles.

The Success of Failure was written to help organizations and individuals create a development path for the growing numbers of young leaders. The book starts the journey by building a foundation from within. It stems from the basic belief that you can't believe in others unless you believe in yourself. You can't accept failure unless you're comfortable failing. Without addressing some of our beliefs and actions, we can't truly help others around us.

The Success of Failure addresses these foundational issues. It also allows you to walk away with key insights and simple ways to address common issues pertaining to how you view yourself and how those beliefs impact your actions. As you work to build your belief in yourself, you alter the perceptions others have of you as a leader and an individual.

ACKNOWLEDGMENTS

I'm so grateful to my wife, Quinn, who was an amazing partner in this endeavor. Her constant encouragement and support ensured this book would get into your hands. And to the rest of the crew at home, Aden, Will, and Jacob, thank you for cheering for me along the way, even if I had to miss some weekday nights and weekend mornings with you.

To my parents, who always encouraged me to go after whatever I wanted. My mom, Andrea, took on the challenge of eliminating my grammar and spelling errors to help me make the early draft presentable. My brother and sister-in-law, Nick and Nicole, were brave enough to provide critiques and encouragement to give the book some real meat. And to the rest of my family, even though this idea initially seemed like just another crazy idea I had, you welcomed the idea and supported me every step of the way.

Thank you, Mike Sale, for sharing your entrepreneurial mind to help me improve each draft of this book. Our MBAs have continued to pay off in spades. To the Newgrange 7 team, you helped me look beyond the book and held me accountable through each step of this process.

Vicki Adang, your work in shaping and editing this book helped me tremendously in crossing the finish line. Thank you to David Hancock and the Morgan James team in helping me bring this work to life. Jenni Robbins, your introduction couldn't have been better timed!

And my gratitude to everyone on the FirstPerson team for your support of this endeavor as well as my own professional growth over these past years.

And to everyone who contributed to this story and the overall lesson, your willingness to share and listen helped bring this lesson to life!

INTRODUCTION

"I can't do it."

"It will never get better."

"Why would anyone want me?"

We say these words about ourselves and our careers. It doesn't matter if we're young or old. Male or female. Financially free or living paycheck to paycheck. These are familiar thoughts. And once spoken, we take these words to heart. We repeat them over and over again.

We don't know when the words first entered our vocabulary. All we know is that we believe them. They have become habit. As smoking creates a cough to compensate for the impact on the lungs, we compensate for our habits in how we work and live.

And when we think we've failed, we seem to fixate on the failure, which adds fuel to the fire. All of a sudden, the perceived failure defines us. It makes us a failure.

This book is for those who are looking to break that habit. To find ways to move on. To say other words that help us grow. To believe we can accomplish what we want. And to know what we are capable of in our lives.

Perhaps you have been in this spot before or you are there now. This book is to help you get out of that spot, out of your own head, and onto a new path.

THE DECISION

All of Tony's big decisions happened in the shower. However, after minute thirty-two, he found himself no clearer than when he started. The ice-cold water flowing from the showerhead wasn't forcing the issue. Shivering in the shower, he was determined to continue until he had an answer.

Two days ago he received a job offer. Not just any offer, but *the* offer. Tony had been keeping his eye on this company since its launch just two years ago. He had introduced himself to the founder. He had kept in touch with the CEO. Tony didn't believe in fate, but he knew he was in the right place at the right time. And while most people would be thrilled at the chance to work at the fastest growing tech firm in town, Tony had been anything but thrilled for the last forty-eight hours.

The offer itself wasn't an issue. In fact, it was exactly what Tony had envisioned—the right role, the right team, the right pay (if there was such a thing).

You know you're going to take it. Kate texted him after she got the news. After a year of dating, she knew Tony's painful decision-making process all too well. She had seen him go through this before, including when she had patiently waited for him to ask her out for the first time.

Despite his struggles with decisions, Tony had built a strong reputation during his young career. Immediately after college, he did what both of his parents said he should do, which was to find a job with a large and stable company that he could grow with. Even though he was young, he was eager. He quickly learned the various roles thrown at him and navigated his way into one of the more senior project management positions after only eighteen months. After two years in the role, Tony realized he'd have to give up another decade of his life to make the next jump up the corporate ladder. So despite his parents' wishes, he gave up their dream and found a small technology startup to join. As employee number ten, he helped hire the next ten and then the next ten. By the time the company signed a buyout deal nearly four years later, Tony was playing a significant role managing the product development side of the firm. Given the fast-paced environment at the company, he never technically managed anyone. Instead, he relied on his ability to easily connect with others to turn big ideas into real and meaningful outcomes.

But this role would be different. He would have to update his LinkedIn profile to say vice president. And the title would mean something because he would be leading such a large part of the business and the people responsible for its day-to-day operations. He wondered if they'd call him "Boss."

"You're pretty lucky," he said to himself. "You've always been at the right place at the right time. Thank goodness you've had other people around you. Otherwise, you wouldn't be here. But your luck is bound to run out soon."

The numbing of his back from the cold water stopped those thoughts. He asked himself one more time, *What's it going to be?*

He turned off the water.

DUCK

It was a cool spring morning. Tony walked down the street with his hands in his pockets and his earbuds in position. Born and raised in Nashville, he was quick to find the latest hot releases in town. He focused on the music spilling into his brain rather than the nervous feeling he had throughout his body.

He remembered the last time he was viewed as the new guy. It had been a few years, but Tony knew the first-day drill: signing paperwork, awkward introductions, and more paperwork. But whatever Tony had imagined happening on his first day at Gr8Lyf (pronounced "great life"), he couldn't have been prepared for what he saw as he entered the lobby.

BANG!

Tony ducked to the floor, closing his eyes. Thinking either a car had just hit the building or the floor above had collapsed, he slowly opened his eyes to see confetti raining down from the ceiling and a familiar face holding what looked like a simple piece of PVC pipe.

"It's a potato gun," the man said, as if that explained everything. "I made it myself. Do you like it?"

"I love it," Tony said, slowly rising from the floor. "Do you shoot at all your employees, or only on their first day?"

"I can't shoot at the people I pay. You're early and not on the payroll yet."

The two men warmly shook hands. "I'm so glad you're here," the man said. "You're in the right place now," he added, still holding the handshake.

The man was Jack Allan, CEO at Gr8Lyf. Jack was on his second midlife crisis, even though he had only recently passed fifty. His first life had been spent successfully creating two companies. Both focused on the nebulous world of online marketing; even he at times found it difficult to tell the difference between the two. He would joke that was why he ultimately sold off both firms.

This time around, he was like a kid in a candy shop. The charismatic smile that shined out from his well-trimmed stubble told everyone around him that he was going to win. Again.

"It's how I greet all my new hires. Here, let me show you around."

"You have some confetti stuck in your shirt," said a soft voice. "Here, let me help."

"Thank you," Tony replied, rubbing his head as he felt for any other pieces that might have been hiding.

"I'm Lori, by the way. You're our new VP, right?"

Tony nodded slowly, almost unsure of how to respond. He knew he would need to get used to that title eventually.

"You'd better get used to ducking around here. He shoots people all the time!"

FAMILIAR FACES

Jack walked Tony through the lobby and into the main office, which was a loose term. The area looked like the company had set up base camp at the bottom of Mt. Everest. Desks were clustered together as if the employees might need to huddle together to keep each other warm. Some groups were focused on their computers, while others huddled in deep conversation on couches they had pulled over to their workspace. Tony took in the view of the surrounding neighborhood buildings, the river below, and the early spring sun shining through it all. He found the entire scene almost magical.

Gr8Lyf was located in a part of town that was emerging from its own midlife crisis. Ten years ago, the area was a sleepy strip of road with a few businesses surrounded by homes. In part because of the successful efforts of Jack and other community leaders, the neighborhood was now a top hot spot for small businesses. Walk south and you'd find the latest food trends mixed with the local flare of Nashville B&B (barbecue and beer) stops. These up-and-coming restaurants rivaled the taste of what you could find downtown, but without the tourist feel. Head north and you'd find a greater mix of choices along with fashion stops that catered to the outdoorsman and working professionals.

While great food and music were the heart of the city, companies like Gr8Lyf were helping Nashville become known for more than that. They were making sure the heart kept beating by recruiting young professionals to the area and keeping them in town. Still considered a startup, Gr8Lyf had received so much local and regional recognition for its technology innovations that city officials pointed to the company as a reason for Nashville's enhanced reputation.

Jack snapped Tony out of his trance by reintroducing him to a familiar face.

"Who let this guy in?" said Kyle.

"You did, or have you forgotten already?" Tony replied quickly.

"That's right. I guess I do have my faults," Kyle said with a smile.

Kyle and Tony had met during their first job out of college. New to the company and the working world, they instantly bonded as more of a survival tactic than anything else. Kyle was great at opening doors and making connections throughout the bureaucracy of the corporate firm for which they worked. Tony knew how to put puzzle pieces together to make sure the products delivered for clients. That made Kyle look good, and his bosses took notice. As Kyle grew within the company to eventually lead the department, which included sales and product development, Tony followed close behind with his own success. Kyle always ribbed Tony that he wouldn't have been anywhere without him.

When Tony left, Kyle continued to grow in the company and led record-making achievements over the next two years. Kyle's success often led him to tease Tony that he had held him back.

As the men's careers grew stronger, so did their relationship. They started exercising together, finally landing on running after an unsuccessful attempt at CrossFit. Tony had been the best man at Kyle's wedding just over a year ago. And Kyle had introduced Kate to Tony. It only made sense that the two were working together again.

Kyle's business card read "Vice President of Customer Opportunities." Although Gr8Lyf attempted to steer clear of overinflated titles, it was an awkward way of saying Kyle led all sales, business development, and marketing efforts as well as the people who supported those functions.

"I'm really excited you're here," Kyle said.

"I'm sure you are," Tony replied. "What did you screw up this time?"

Kyle laughed and looked at the floor. When he looked up, his face was serious. "No, I mean it. You're going to have a real positive impact here. You said so yourself. Right, Dave?"

Tony looked behind him to see Dave Whitney walk up. Unlike the others Tony had met that morning, Dave wasn't engrossed in his phone or computer. Rather, he held a small leather-bound notebook, with a pen that acted as a bookmark. He was the oldest employee in the company, which wasn't a hard-won honor at Gr8Lyf. Even Tony felt old looking around at the younger faces in the company. If Tony had to guess, Dave would be close to his father's age.

"I did say that. Welcome aboard, Tony." Dave greeted Tony with an outstretched hand. "And it looks like you're already settling in if you're putting Kyle in his place."

Tony laughed. "Thanks, Dave. It's a real pleasure to be able to work with you and the team."

Dave's fingerprints were on nearly all of Nashville's most successful ventures. He had personally started, funded, or helped manage multiple companies over the last thirty years. And although Dave's reputation in town was strong and successful, it was for very different reasons than the other leaders of his caliber. Dave preferred playing a supporting role rather than being in the CEO's spotlight. Because of this, Tony hadn't had much interaction with Dave. Even during Tony's interviews, Dave was quiet, preferring to take notes in his notebook instead of add to the stories the others told. When Tony did hear Dave speak, he was purposeful and thoughtful in the questions he asked and comments he made. Tony found his interviewing style one of the hardest parts of his interview process. Most everyone, including Jack, treated the interview as a sort of social hour. During Tony's meeting with his potential team, they talked more about who had traveled the most rather than about the role or Tony's leadership style. But Tony was intimidated when he met with Dave. Part of it was the age difference and the accomplishments Dave had achieved in his career. But the questions Dave asked during the ninety minutes they spent together were direct and almost personal. His questions focused on Tony's experiences and results. Because talking about himself was one of his least favorite things to do, Tony was uncomfortable with his responses. But Dave's demeanor made it somehow bearable, even enjoyable. Tony was looking forward to getting to know him better.

MEETING THE TEAM

"And here is our new VP of Customer Awesomeness," Jack yelled to another corner of the floor. As they approached, Tony could see six people huddled together in front of one computer. It was his new team.

"Good morning," Tony said, worried he was interrupting something important. He tried to remind himself that he was going to have to get past that, but the size of the group sent a visual reminder of how overwhelmed he was with the idea of managing this team.

The group jumped up, as if the approaching footsteps had woken them from a trance. They each turned around and stood at attention. Tony would have thought of the group as an army platoon if it hadn't been for the oversized nose-and-glasses disguises they wore.

"Yes, sir!" they shouted.

Jack leaned over to Tony. "This was not my idea," he whispered.

They were lined up tallest to shortest. "Roll call," shouted the tallest.

As they rattled off their names, Tony felt more at ease with the fun nature of the group. He put his hands behind his back and stuck out his chest. He walked back and forth in front of the line, looking each person up and down. He was enjoying the bit and playing along. When the last person finished, it was Tony's turn to do the shouting.

"Thank you," Tony barked in the best military general voice he could muster. "I'm impressed by your ability to remember your own names and what you do. I hope you'll help me remember what I'm supposed to do with the title I have."

The group laughed. They, along with Tony, thought his new title was silly as well.

Tony softened. "Thank you for the fun welcome. I'm really looking forward to getting to know each of you and helping Gr8Lyf go to the next level."

At that, a loud horn sounded, as if they were at a hockey game and the home team had just scored a goal.

Tony gave a confused look—something he was quickly getting used to.

"You look lost," said Molly, one of his team members who approached him as the group broke formation. Tony remembered her from the group interview right away. She had lived in nearly half of the countries in Europe during her role as a consultant with IBM. Her resume was intimidating, yet her demeanor was anything but.

I feel like I don't belong here, Tony thought to himself.

"Yes. What was that noise?" he said to Molly.

"It's time for morning standup. Don't worry; first days can be tough," she said.

MORNING STANDUP

Tony and Molly joined another team member, Robert, as they walked down the hallway. In contrast to Molly's professional experiences, Robert had started his own company before he joined Gr8Lyf. It was a success for everyone except Robert. Although he had sold the company at a very nice price more than three years ago, he still believed it could have been something bigger.

"If only I had known you were looking," Robert said to Tony. "We could have been something!"

"Let it go, Robert," Molly said, rolling her eyes and looking at Tony. "He can't let it go. He's just glad there is someone new here to listen to his stories."

Tony laughed awkwardly. He had prepared himself for being the new guy, but even so, this much attention was starting to wear on him. And it was only 9:15 a.m.

Robert didn't let it go. As he talked about his last company, he explained how he believed he was living his second life. While he still dreamed of what could have been with his creation, he was now content to help other entrepreneurs, like Jack, in whatever role they needed—even if it meant taking on the role of a utility player.

"Well, I'm sure the team looks up to you, given everything you've accomplished," said Tony. Robert's resume and list of accomplishments were impressive. Tony found himself wondering how he had landed this role instead of Robert. Or Molly. Or anyone else for that matter.

"Don't tell him we look up to him," Molly quipped. "We don't need his head to get any bigger."

Robert rolled his eyes. "We're in here," he said.

Most of the other employees, just over forty of them, had gathered in the room by the time the trio arrived. For as open as the office was, this room was much different.

"Well, this is tight," Tony said out loud without realizing it. Molly and Robert didn't notice the comment, but the constant shuffling of feet made it apparent that everyone in the room would have agreed with him. The tight quarters gave a feeling that they were meeting in a closet. Tony did have to admit that without chairs, the space seemed workable for the meeting. The one chair that was in the room was being used by Jack, who was standing on it.

"OK. Big day today. Let's get started. Can somebody start the clock?" Jack said.

Tony looked up and saw 15:00 appear on a mini-scoreboard and then start to tick down second by second.

"Happy Monday, everyone. I'm really excited to introduce our newest member of the team. He's been stalking us for a number of years, and I'm glad to say that we've been doing the same."

Jack paused. After he got the laughs he was looking for, he started again. “We are very lucky to have him, and he’s going to help us go even further toward our vision. Tony, please say hello and give us some insight into that great brain of yours.”

Tony took a deep breath as Jack finished. Speaking in front of a large crowd wasn’t unusual for him, but he would have preferred plenty of other tasks.

“Thank you, Jack. And thank you all. I am slightly embarrassed that my infatuation in what you all have been doing over the last two years is now public. I tried to keep it a secret, but I’m glad the word is out. It’s been amazing to watch Gr8Lyf grow during that time, and I am super-excited to be part of the future.”

The group gave Tony a kind round of applause as Tony looked back at Jack.

“Great. Thank you, Tony. Kyle, how are we looking?”

As Kyle gave an update on sales, Tony scanned the room. He looked at Robert, who gave him a thumbs-up. Then he saw Molly talking to another woman on his team. They were whispering and looking in his direction.

Oh, no, thought Tony. *I did sound like an idiot. I can’t believe you didn’t mention your team. What were you thinking? You weren’t, that’s the problem. It’s your first day, and you’re already messing up.*

Tony tried to bring himself back to the meeting. The clock read 4:48 left in the meeting. Kyle was still talking. Tony looked at him and then back to the crowd. Molly was now deeply drawn into her phone. Others were looking to Jack as if he were talking. Nobody seemed to notice that Kyle was sharing some pivotal company information, let alone that he was in the room.

Tony decided to speak up. “Kyle, I know I’m the new guy, but can you tell me what you’re hearing from our current clients regarding our upcoming product launch?”

Kyle paused and looked at Jack, who was starting to respond. "Great question, Tony. Clients have said they like the direction we are planning to take. It makes sense for us. And given the investment in our operations, that's a good thing for you and your new role."

Tony laughed as he got the meaning of the joke. His role was new to the organization and a sign that they were investing in the future. Tony enjoyed getting into the weeds; it had made him successful in past roles. And he could tell when someone didn't have the detail he was looking for. Tony opened his mouth to ask another question, but as he did, Jack cut him off.

"We can catch the new guy up later so we don't waste everyone else's time," he said. "Natalie, can you give everyone a quick update on our financials?"

Tony's smile slowly faded as the meeting moved on.

I told you not to ask that question. You really know how to start off on the wrong foot.

THE WALK HOME

Sitting on the park bench outside Gr8Lyf's office, Kate was checking her phone, waiting for an update from Tony. She was growing impatient. She knew it was his first day, but at 6:30 p.m., she was also starting to get nervous. She texted again.

Should I head to the bar?

They had agreed to grab a drink before they each headed off for the evening. Kate led a late-night yoga class. Tony was planning to meet up with a former college roommate who was looking for help with his own career. Left to his own devices, Tony wouldn't have celebrated his first day at a new job. Kate had demanded it, saying she wanted to recognize the day.

"You've worked hard for this," she would say after a major accomplishment. "You need to do something nice for yourself."

Tony's response was always the same: "I'll celebrate when I actually do something. Just getting hired isn't anything special."

"Nothing special?" Kate would reply. "Gr8Lyf only hires the best. You should be proud of yourself."

After killing fifteen more minutes on Instagram, Kate still hadn't heard from Tony. As she stood up to cross the street, she saw him walk out the door.

"Everything OK?" she asked as he quickly kissed her cheek.

"I'm sorry. Jack needed to share some things with me before I left. Are we too late before your class?"

"Yes. But someone can cover for me if we can't get out on time. You think you can keep up?"

His smirk acknowledged his acceptance of her challenge.

"So how did it go?"

"Fine," Tony replied as he nodded his head.

Kate smiled. She was prepared for this response. She had dated Tony long enough to learn this habit of his. Early in the relationship, she thought he was keeping things from her. It took her some time to learn that "fine" was his way of thinking through things. Tony was fine after he lost his wallet on their first date. He was fine after he helped his former company close its acquisition deal. Fine was only scratching at the surface.

"Oh yeah? What was fine about it?" she asked.

Tony exhaled. "It was a nice first day. There is just lots of work to do."

"I'm sure. Are they on track in launching the new product? It sounds like it'll be big."

Kate had no clue what she was even asking, but as an event planner, she had learned the right ways to ask the right questions. She had been around the tech community long enough to know what to ask and listen for.

"We didn't get into it much." Tony was picking up the pace.

"And how's your team? They seemed nice from what you told me last time."

"They're amazingly talented. Talking to each of them, it's hard to believe they've struggled to complete this product."

"Good thing you're there," Kate said, trying to pick up the conversation along with the pace.

"There are just so many of them. I've never had to manage so many people."

"I'm sure you'll do great," said Kate, matching his stride. "And you'll be able to help them finish the product."

"They hired me to do more than just that," Tony said shortly.

"Oh really?" Kate asked with a smirk while biting her tongue. Her patience as he went through this process only lasted so long. She could draw out only so much from him before she would eventually get frustrated. She spent the next block walking in silence.

"I'm sorry. I just have a lot on my mind. The expectations, timeline, and the team are just bigger than I realized. Trying to sort it all out in my head."

"I get it," Kate said, looking past him. "How's Kyle?" she asked, hoping to move onto another topic.

"Fine," he said.

FIRST LOOK

The rest of the week felt like a blur to Tony. He quickly got into the thick of things, given his hands-on approach, but he also had an eye on the critical timing of the product launch. Not knowing the best way to connect with his team, he drew on what had worked well in his previous roles, which was to get the other person talking. He met one on one with each of his team members and focused the discussion on three areas: what was going well, what needed improvement, and what they needed from him. After the conversations, Tony still felt out of his league in having to manage the group of high performers, but he was somewhat relieved to hear that even they were struggling to accomplish their team goals together. He was beginning to think that he might find a few ways to add value to the team.

Tony was given an opportunity at his first product development team meeting. The topic was the product launch, which was top of mind for everyone. Because Tony had connected with everyone before the meeting, he knew the issues and the concerns people had. They were as anxious as he was to make the launch a success. But in the first ten minutes of the meeting, Tony quickly caught onto the difficulties his talented team members had communicating with each other. The meeting started with no agenda, and Molly and Robert did all of the talking early on. Tony quietly interjected by asking questions that pulled others into the conversation. Within the next ten minutes, Tony felt everyone had been given a chance to add something to the conversation, rather than waiting for permission to speak. By the end of the meeting, the group was able to agree on the expectations moving forward.

"That was amazing. I wonder what was so awesome about me today," Robert said as the group departed.

Molly rolled her eyes. "Thanks, Tony. It's about time you got here."

Tony nodded, acknowledging them both before he went to his next meeting. It was the leadership team's first opportunity to meet. Jack had explained how he used these meetings to set the stage for Gr8Lyf's future, not just with the new product launch, but in looking toward what he wanted the company to become in the years ahead. The leadership team's ability to think big picture was one of the things that had drawn Tony to the company. Typically not a fan of meetings, he was excited for this one.

Jack occupied a large corner office, taking up more space than one would expect, given the open floor space in the rest of the office. The amount of furniture and other random pieces seemed to exist only to show that the amount of space was warranted. The large oval table near the two large corner windows was surrounded by sports and music memorabilia.

A large couch along one of the windows served as meeting spot during the day and a bed for Jack some nights. Although he had a large apartment overlooking the Broadway strip downtown, he found it easier to sleep in the office on some late nights.

"It was all my wife would let me have after the divorce," Jack said to Tony as he looked at the couch. "I've had it for years. It helps me think."

Kyle and Dave walked into the office in mid-conversation. Kyle was nodding, and his shoulders were slightly hunched. Kyle was one of the most positive guys Tony knew, but now he looked more tired than he typically would for a 10 a.m. meeting.

"You've been here before," Tony heard Dave say. "You can do it again." Dave seemed to be whispering so as not to disturb the others.

"Everything OK?" Jack asked as he looked at his computer.

Both of them nodded.

"Shall we get started?" Dave asked as he sat down.

Jack eyed Kyle and Dave, looking from one to the other, waiting for an explanation. "OK," he said with a shrug. He realized he wasn't going to get the story he wanted.

"Tony, since you're the new guy, it might be helpful to give you some background on these meetings. Agreed?" Jack said.

Tony nodded. Tony thought a three-hour meeting with no agenda was never a good sign, so he was pleased to be offered some insight.

Jack began. "These meetings are an opportunity for this team to connect and work on the business and not in the business. It is a time to think forward rather than in the moment."

Tony nodded again. He still wondered what that would entail, but released the need to satisfy his growing curiosity.

"So where should we start, gang?"

Dave and Kyle looked at each other. Their looks seemed to acknowledge the need to pick up where they had left off in their earlier conversation.

Dave broke the silence. "Perhaps it might be helpful to give insight into some of the areas we discussed before Tony joined the team?"

"Great idea, Dave," Jack responded. He stood up and went to the whiteboard. For the next thirty minutes, Jack talked about the last twelve months at Gr8Lyf. As he talked, he made two lists. The first were accomplishments over the last year. Continued increase in revenue and client reach fell within the short list of successes. What surprised Tony was the list of items that Jack called challenges. By the time Jack reached the bottom of the whiteboard, Tony counted eighteen challenges compared to only four accomplishments.

"What have I missed?" Jack asked, looking at Kyle and Dave.

Kyle had sunk lower in his seat since Jack first started. He was looking down at the table and tapping his pen very slowly. Most of the challenges were related to sales, although product development had its share. Tony was surprised by how poorly Jack viewed the organization's performance. Typically, he was very optimistic, using buzzwords such as "collaborative" and "innovative" to describe the team. But just now, Jack had used words like "disjointed," "slow," and "archaic." Tony looked at Kyle as Jack talked. It seemed the weight of those words had pushed him lower in his chair.

Dave looked at Kyle and then back at Jack. "I'm surprised by the two lists. It feels like we're missing a few successes." Dave made the statement as if giving Kyle an opportunity to jump in. Kyle nodded, but remained silent.

"I think we need to be careful about not taking small wins as larger successes," Jack replied. "We take on our challenges and don't hide from them."

"Agreed," Dave said. "But we also need to be honest in assessing them. Given what we have accomplished this past year, is it fair to call our team—or even many of our processes—disjointed?"

"Well." Jack paused for a moment. "What would you call them? How would you describe the fact that our pipeline hasn't grown in the last quarter? Or that client retention continues to remain stagnant? Or that deadlines continue to be missed?"

"We need to be sure to examine the full picture," Dave said. "Kyle's team had a heavy load the last half of the year. And now it's all hands on deck for the product launch and conference. I think part of today's goal was to come back to that pipeline discussion to see what progress Kyle's team has made."

Jack looked at Kyle as a director would look at an actor on stage who had forgotten his lines. Kyle sat up straight in his chair. He cleared his throat, almost hesitant on how to begin, given the tension that was building. Tony knew Kyle was struggling to get his sales team to think longer term, but given the success in the company's growth over the last eighteen months, it was easy to forgive.

Jack took a seat, intently listening to the actions Kyle had taken with his team. From Tony's perspective, Kyle seemed to have implemented a fair mix of new processes and training for his group, along with having heart-to-heart discussions with specific underperforming team members. It appeared to him that Kyle was on top of the situation and his moves were showing progress. However, Jack's expression said otherwise.

As Kyle paused to transition deeper into the topic, Jack stopped him. "So why is this taking so long?" Jack said. "When are you going to get things started? You've been delaying this for too long, Kyle." He then turned to Tony.

"I'm looking for people who can help me lead. Who aren't willing to settle. You've had time to talk with your team. What are you going to do to fix this?"

Tony hadn't come to the meeting with any solutions. Having not even completed a full week, he was thankful he knew where to sit. He did, however, have some ideas about the main issues. His one-on-one and team meetings had allowed him to formulate some thoughts regarding the product as well as the missed deadlines. Jack stopped him before he could finish sharing his discoveries.

"I'm not looking for ideas. I'm looking for answers. When will I get answers?" Jack asked, looking at Kyle and Tony.

Both seemed unsure of how to answer. Kyle committed to having an update for Jack by the end of the weekend. Tony nodded in agreement, knowing that they had planned to go to a cabin for the weekend with a close group of friends.

"OK," Jack responded, sighing heavily. "That wasn't so bad now, was it?"

SOUND CHECK

Tony had been at Gr8Lyf just over a month, but it felt more like six months. Tony had never worked as much or as hard in his career as he had in the last thirty days. He knew his new role was going to be different, but nothing could have prepared him for how different it really was.

Much of the work came from the demands of the product launch. There was so much to do. Tony knew as much when he and Jack talked during the interviews. Jack was determined to have the product ready in time for their annual conference, Lyfrs, in July. He believed that the conference was the place to show the market the company's ability to create and innovate.

Innovation was going to be key with this product. Unlike in his past companies, Jack had invested in a large amount of research and development this time around to create a marketing technology that supported email and website campaigns for some significant online names. The data that Gr8Lyf could provide to these clients would enable them to add more personalization to their messages, and thus more value for their own customers.

Tony and Kyle spent much of the weekend at the cabin creating a solid plan for resolving the remaining product issues. Although their significant others were disappointed the two had missed out on relaxing with their friends, they were relieved to see them both smiling again by the end of the weekend. Despite their quick progress, Tony knew he and his team had only sixty days left to execute the plan.

Something else was contributing to the feeling of running at break-neck speed. He had noticed it in his team, and others as well. Unsure of how to bring up the subject, Tony thought an after-hours get-together might work. After a particularly difficult team meeting, he offered to buy the first round of drinks for his team. Everyone was quick to take him up on the offer.

Robert was thankful for the time. He took a seat next to Tony, who was listening to Molly talk about her weekly volunteer work for a local not-for-profit.

"I'm not sure where you get the energy to do everything you do. After work, I'm wiped," Tony said.

"After I play a show and I put Sally in her bed, I still feel the music," Robert said, interjecting himself into the conversation. Sally, Tony had learned, was Robert's guitar. Robert was one of a few Gr8Lyfrs who played in a band. Those who didn't play followed a local band or two.

"It's similar at Gr8Lyf," Robert continued. "I feel a buzz when I leave work. Part of it is the feeling I get from the work I do. Whether I'm IM'ing at the office or texting with Molly, the buzz stays with me even when I'm not at the office."

Molly and Tony nodded. Even in his short time there, Tony understood. Although he tried to chalk up his daily wiped-out feeling to turning thirty, the ongoing aura of what he and his team were doing followed him throughout his evenings and into the weekends. It was invigorating. He could feel it when he woke up in the morning. It got him out of bed.

"But that buzz can also be tiring," Robert said. "The purpose and the work at Gr8Lyf are invigorating. To be one of the city's leading tech firms is a confidence boost. But the way the company went about getting things done seemed harder than it needed to be."

"What do you chalk that up to?" asked Tony.

"We need to turn down the sound," Robert said. "The acoustics are off or something. There is too much feedback."

"Feedback?" Molly asked.

"I'm not sure I understand," Tony said. Tony's own musical career had been a short one. His second-grade teacher had encouraged him to make a beautiful sound with the recorder. As much as he tried, however, the sound was far from beautiful. She suggested the triangle as the next instrument to try.

"If my band is playing a show and the music that comes out through the speaker system is picked up by the microphone, it is collected and then re-amplified. It begins an infinitely repeating loop that makes that awful sound."

Tony and Molly looked blankly at Robert.

Robert sighed. "We meet to meet. We have meetings about future meetings. And those meetings talk about meetings we just had. I spend most of my day having meetings about other meetings. There's too much feedback."

Tony understood. He was feeling that meeting feedback as well. During his first week, he thought many of the conversations in the meetings he attended were for his benefit. But by the following week, he knew team members weren't having those conversations to be nice. Rather, they were caught in a never-ending feedback loop.

Tony had grown used to this with each company he joined. Call it culture, but every company had something unique. The front end was visible to everyone. It was what the market saw, what clients experienced, and what helped recruit new employees. But behind the scenes, each company possessed its own set of quirks. The challenge was spotting those quirks as soon as possible. Tony was finding that his new role was to help others navigate those quirks and either create ways to overcome those quirks or find ways to work within the uniqueness. His role was to not necessarily break the culture, but enhance it. Meetings were just a small part of the problem. He would also have to keep his team focused on the things that mattered.

"So what are you going to do about it?" Molly asked him.

Tony laughed awkwardly, asking himself the same question.

BREAKTHROUGH

Tony sipped his second cup of coffee as he read the text from Jack.

Running late c u in 15.

Jack had a habit of scheduling these early morning meetings, deemed mission critical, only to change his perception of urgency as the meeting time finally arrived. Tony had picked up on the custom by now and was content to enjoy his coffee while catching up on some people watching. He rubbed the week-old growth on his face, wondering if it might be time to shave.

During the week, this coffee shop was uniquely built for doing business. Whether striking a deal, meeting a new connection, or catching up with a colleague, the hippie staff, rustic atmosphere, and odd breakfast items combined to make the experience complete. From the outside, a passerby would think this was a spot for a Vandy student to swing by and kill a morning or even the whole day. Perhaps it was the $12 vegan omelets that scared students away, but there was an unspoken rule that this was a place to do business.

Tony went to refill his cup, walking past the refurbished hardwood tables where patrons sat. The lighting in the shop was warm but low, almost designed to help people wake up as the sun started to rise. Tony poured coffee from the self-service bar; even he was surprised at how much coffee he had been drinking in the last few weeks.

"Grab one for me too," yelled Jack as he walked through the door. Many of the staff greeted him as if they were welcoming him into his own home. Rightfully so, as Jack had closed some of his biggest deals here. And the staff was always prepared to make sure he had what he needed to celebrate.

Tony and Jack sat down at a table near a large window overlooking the neighborhood street. The view outside showed occasional walkers and runners passing by. It was late spring, but the warm, humid air gave the impression it was summer.

"I need to start scheduling these meetings later, don't I?" asked Jack.

"Nah. You're fine. Maybe the downtown lifestyle is getting to you?" Tony said jokingly.

"I can't give that up. I haven't had this much fun in years."

If Jack's first life was marked by the success of building and selling his two firms, his second life began after his divorce. Although he didn't open up about the details, he was quick to confirm he had made the right decision. He would talk about his new lifestyle as if it were newly found freedom. And he would frequently ask Tony and others in the company to join him in some of his late-night adventures. Even though Tony was nearly twenty years younger, he found it hard to keep up with Jack. He learned to pace himself on the evenings out and would rely on his relationship with Kate as an out.

"You'll join me next time, right?" Jack asked.

"Sure. Should we dig in?" Tony asked, moving on to the work at hand.

"Yes. I heard you say breakthrough at our last meeting. You seemed excited. Tell me about it."

"Excited is a strong word, but perhaps hopeful?" Tony tried to hide his optimism about being able to launch the new product on time. He knew there was still a lot of work to do, but he allowed a small smile, acknowledging that things seemed to be on the right track. He dug his laptop out of his backpack and picked up where they had left off in the previous leadership team meeting.

Never before had his former managers asked for so much detail. He grew up with the belief that he should speak only when spoken to. Now Tony was slowly picking up on the need to prepare more than quick, on-the-fly updates. He was finding these types of meetings necessary to give a deeper dive into the facts. Jack seemed to respond well to these meetings, given his fast tempo.

As the computer booted up, Tony talked through how the team had been working incredibly hard over the previous weeks. Although they had encountered some initial bumps, they had identified the source of the issue that the leadership team had picked up on as they looked ahead to the product's launch. After some fine-tuning, Tony explained, he felt they would be in a great spot with the new product in time for the conference.

Tony started walking Jack through the demo, step by step. Tony felt unsure about going through the steps in such painstaking detail. He looked to Jack for reassurance that the detail was necessary. Jack responded with encouraging nods as Tony clicked through each page. As Tony finished, Jack started to sway in his chair, confirming he was seeing what he needed.

"Robert and Molly both really stepped up here," Tony said. "It was impressive to see how they led their teams and worked together during the last month. The team has especially started turning to Molly. Her response has been strong."

"Agreed," Jack said. He was only half-listening; his eyes were still glued to the last page. He was silent except for the sound of a tapping foot on the floor.

"Well done," Jack said finally.

"It was the team," Tony replied. "They are amazing."

"They couldn't have done it without you. You showed them the way."

"I got out of the way." Tony laughed uncomfortably.

"You shouldn't ignore what you're doing for us here. It's not going unnoticed."

"Thank you," Tony said. "How do you feel about the conference now?"

"Better," replied the swaying Jack. "Much better."

TEACHER'S PET

During the week before the conference, the Gr8Lyf office was full of energy. Employees were either running or walking; there was no time for sitting. And no room. Boxes of T-shirts and other giveaways were stacked against any free wall. Marketing banners and stands filled the middle of the room. The way things were stacked gave the feel of being lost in a maze.

The entire team was put to work. Nobody was left without a role. For the large number of employees who had worked on the conference last year, this was routine. They referred to this period as hell week. Those new to the experience, including Tony, quickly learned why.

Although not an employee of Gr8Lyf, Kate already knew why it had earned that name. She and her team had been the event planner for the conference last year. Although they had led larger events in terms of cost and number of participants, the Lyfrs conference was the most grueling. She had lost one of her best employees after the event, given the high level of chaos and small margin of error. The fact that Tony was being solicited allowed Kate to pass on the event this year, saying she'd didn't want to create a conflict of interest. She missed the paycheck that came with the conference but not the drama.

Kate's experience gave Tony the excuse to be absent from her for the better part of the week. He had been understanding last year during the last-minute changes; now it was her turn to support him from the sidelines.

Morning standup was about to start. Tony could hear the other employees grumbling that there wasn't enough time to meet. They had too much to do. Tony smiled at the comments. Yes, they were complaining, but to him it meant they knew what the priority was and didn't want anything to get in the way. But this meeting had a purpose. Tony was going to introduce the new product to the entire company before the public got a glimpse of it at the conference.

The clock started counting down, and Jack got started.

"We've all put in a lot of hours, sweat, and tears this year. We are less than a week away from the market and our competitors seeing what we can really accomplish. Since our beginning, we have been playing in the minor league. With Tony's leadership, the team has made great strides on a product that we have struggled with for too long."

Tony heard a compliment somewhere in there but wasn't sure it was the message the group needed to hear. The team appeared to feel the same way. Their eyes were cast straight at the ground. Tony began to speak, but Jack continued.

"Our competitors have beaten us on so many issues. We have been behind the times in this area since our beginning, but now Tony has led us to the promised land."

Tony felt like he needed to pull a fire alarm to put a stop to Jack's comments, but he was frozen watching this all unfold.

"Tony, I can't wait for you to show us what you've created."

"Thanks, Jack," Tony said, relieved. "And thank you for the vision and leadership you've provided to us to get to this point. Before I begin, I want to call out real leaders. Molly, Robert, and the entire team have done remarkable things together. They took this idea and made it into reality. I was able to be close enough to the action to see it all happen."

Tony turned the floor over to Molly to start the demo. Typically she wasn't a slow start when in front of a crowd. As he watched her struggle in her opening comments, Tony couldn't help but feel that Jack's comments may have been damaging, which was causing her lack of enthusiasm.

As she finished the demo, Tony took the opportunity to recognize his team one more time and throw a nod of appreciation to Jack. As the buzzer sounded, the team slowly departed, trying not to make eye contact with each other.

Tony immediately went to Molly, who was talking Robert. "I didn't know he would do that," he said.

"That's OK," Molly said as she shrugged. "It was nothing."

"I'm really sorry." Tony was at a loss for words.

Robert looked at Tony. "Just be careful. The teacher's pet always gets hit the hardest."

Before Tony could ask what that meant, Jack walked up and slapped him on the back.

"I can't wait until next week!" Jack said.

As the others exited, Jack and Tony were left alone in the room.

"I wish I had more time to recognize the team," Tony said, staring at Jack. "They did some really great work."

"They sure did. You should make sure you acknowledge that soon. You wouldn't want them to feel that they were missed."

AFTER-PARTY

The conference's biggest draw was the final event of the week. Conference-goers anticipated this unofficial get-together as much as they had looked forward to some of the week's top speakers.

This year's party, as had been done in the past, was held at a location as inconvenient to out-of-town travelers as possible. The original intent was to provide employees and local partners an opportunity to unwind after a long week. But legend had grown enough for return participants to plan for the event. This year, only a small percentage of attendees had not planned ahead for an extra night of socializing.

Tony was huddled around a table with many of his team, listening to a heated debate between Robert and Alyssa, a local marketing guru.

"I don't know anyone who is as far along as we are on this idea," stated Robert. He had tossed back a few beers, which made him believe even more strongly in his stance.

Alyssa took the opposing view. "I wouldn't get too excited. You have others who are close, if not slightly ahead. You've been moving in the right direction, but it has taken you awhile to get here." She would know. She had worked with Gr8Lyf as a consultant during the company's first year.

"I don't know how you could say that," Molly jumped in. "We've been moving at light speed."

"Yes, you have. But you've stalled out at times. You need to keep this pace up and not lose momentum built from this week."

"How do you mean?" asked Robert. "The conference was an enormous success. Attendance was not only at a record level, but those who attended were engaged. Kyle's still counting, but according to him, the number of qualified leads that came through from the week skyrocketed compared to last year." Robert was standing by this point. "We kicked this conference in the—"

Tony saw Molly roll her eyes. She looked back at Tony to share a laugh. They found it easier to let Robert go down in an argument like this on his own.

"What I mean," interrupted Alyssa, "is that you've done this before. Gr8Lyf is known for having great ideas, only to not follow through on them. You all talk a great game, but delivery runs short."

"Oh yeah?" Robert was trying to stare at Alyssa, but he was starting to lose his balance. "We have this guy," Robert said, pointing to Tony. "He's going to deliver!"

"We're going to deliver," said Tony. "Until then, what does everyone need?" He used the attention to excuse himself from the conversation.

"I love you, man," said Robert.

"I love you too. But one more and then you're done. OK?"

Robert nodded and tried to wink, but tilted his body so much he fell into his chair. "You know what? I think you're right. I'm good!"

The group started smacking Robert with the small pillows that were laying in each of their chairs. Tony left, not wanting to get caught in the crossfire. He pointed himself toward the bar and found Kyle talking to three people. Their faces didn't look familiar, but given the amount of new clients and partners he had met during the conference, he wasn't surprised. As he got closer, he saw Kyle hand out shots to each of them.

"I can't believe you all came all this way. I can't tell you how much we appreciate all of your support." Kyle saw Tony walking up. "And speaking of appreciation, here is the man of the hour! Tony, say hello to our best customer."

"I'm sure you say that to all your customers, Kyle," said one of the two women in the group.

"I mean it! You're the best customer. At this bar. Right now," Kyle said with a smile.

"Is he causing you trouble?" asked Tony.

"No, we know how to handle him," said the other woman. "So Kyle says you're the brains behind the new product."

"I wouldn't say that," Tony said quickly. "If you know Kyle, you know who is really in charge."

"I'll drink to that," Kyle responded, holding up his glass and tossing back his drink.

The woman smiled at the passed compliment and then asked, "But do you think you can help see this one through?"

"How do you mean?" asked Tony.

"Go easy on him, Sharon," warned Kyle. "He's still a newbie in our world."

Sharon paused and stared at Tony, as if readjusting her focus. "Don't get me wrong," she said. "Gr8Lyf is doing wonderful things. I wouldn't trade your team for anything in the world. I know what to expect. You're going to provide great service every day, and you're going to find new ways to help me be successful. But at some point, you're going to need to deliver on those new ideas. You're going to need to not just talk, but get it done."

For the second time that night, Tony was surprised, but looked at Kyle and saw him nodding.

"This is the one, Sharon," Kyle said as he slowly slapped Tony on the back three times. "This is the one."

MOMENTUM

Tony exhaled into the cold November morning air, leaving a puff of his breath behind him as he ran down the road. It was one of the first truly cold mornings, confirming that winter was making an early arrival this year.

"So how much more than last month?" he asked.

"Nearly threefold," said Kyle. "Since the product officially launched in July, we've just been killing it."

They had started running together after Kyle injured himself in a CrossFit class they were taking together. They found that mornings were the only way to stay committed to each other. Shortly after the wedding, Kyle and his wife had bought a home, which came with a long list of repairs that filled his time after work. Their weekly morning ritual was a way to stay connected on work and life issues.

Work topics typically won out, and the last four months since the conference were no exception.

The conference had generated the excitement and buzz Gr8Lyf was looking for with its new product, and the official launch went off with the same fanfare a few weeks later. Initial reviews were glowing, and sales had grown rapidly over the last three months. Kyle was right; they were killing it.

"I don't think anyone could have prepared us for this reaction. It's been amazing," Kyle said. "How are you guys coming along on the first update?"

"Fine," said Tony. "We've gotten the early bugs resolved, and we'll be able to release the update by the end of the year."

Since the initial release, Tony and his team had been keeping an eye on the main issue that had troubled the product from the beginning. It was a standard topic for the leadership team meetings as well. Although the fix that was implemented seemed to do the job, the product itself had produced some minor but nagging issues. The issue that had started as a main topic was starting to slowly move down everyone's priority list. Even Tony had become resigned to the progress the team was making.

"Are you hearing anything?"

"Nope." Kyle had been through enough releases in the past to know this was part of the process. "How are things going with Kate? When are you going to make her an honest woman?"

"I still need to pick out the ring. The timing needs to be right, too."

"For you, dude, the timing will never be right. You need to make the time right. What are you waiting for?"

"We've been together for barely three years. Don't you think we need more time than that?"

"But you've known her for longer than that. It took you forever just to ask her out. Give yourself some credit, brother."

Kyle was right. Again. Tony had spent an entire summer debating whether to ask Kate out. Kyle had refused to run with him until he made a move. He couldn't go through the same round of questioning: Should I ask her out? What do you think she would say? What would she see in me? Kyle called it whining, but to Tony, those seemed like decent questions to ask.

"Hold up at that stop sign, Tony. I'm getting a text."

They approached their halfway point. During the day, this was a busy intersection. However, at this early hour, it was almost peaceful.

"You still run with that thing? I thought you gave up being connected all the time."

"I need to. Clients are all over me; I'm not going to pass this time up," Kyle said as he pulled out his phone.

"It's from the folks at Mixly."

"How are they doing?"

Mixly was one of the initial adopters of the new product. They were a long-time customer of Gr8Lyf and their largest customer. They had direct access to Jack and anyone else on the Gr8Lyf team, given their size and local presence. And they were always willing and quick to reach out.

"They say it's urgent. I'll catch you at the office, OK?"

"Sounds good. Good luck!" Tony yelled over his shoulder as he headed in the opposite direction at the intersection.

A CRACK IN THE SYSTEM

Tony thought it was strange that he hadn't heard back from Kyle by the time he arrived at the office. They typically stayed close on gathering feedback from clients. Each had a desire to always ensure the customer was happy, even if their roles accomplished that goal in different ways. For anything significant, Kyle was typically the receiver and then deliverer of the news. Tony would then lead the fix and communication back to the client. Given their long-term relationship, it was second nature to keep each other in the loop. They had found through experience that each of them would bring the other into the issue at some point. It was better to be armed with the facts rather than perceptions.

As he walked through the office, Tony's strange feeling wasn't improving. The office was silent, despite the number of employees already at work. He could tell something was up but couldn't put his finger on it.

"Jack has been looking for you," said Lori. She looked almost frantic.

"Jack?" Tony looked at his phone. It was 8:35 a.m. "I haven't heard anything from him. I wonder why he hasn't called."

"I don't know, but you'd better find him."

Tony walked through the office, hoping to find Kyle as well. As much as they stayed connected on client issues, they stayed closer on presenting the information to Jack. Tony found Kyle's desk empty, as were the meeting areas. He asked some of Kyle's team members if they knew his whereabouts but was greeted with shrugs. When he brought up Mixly, they looked equally confused. They said they hadn't seen or heard from Kyle yet. Tony's uneasy feeling was growing by the minute.

Tony started texting Kyle as Jack appeared from around the corner. "Good morning," Jack shouted from across the hall.

Tony returned the greeting and saw right away that something was wrong. Jack's eyes looked bloodshot, as if he had been up for most of the night.

"How are you? Is everything OK?" asked Tony.

"You tell me," snapped Jack as if he had been waiting for that question for some time. "Kyle has been keeping me up to speed on some of the problems that still remain on the new product."

Tony thought back to his recent conversations with Kyle. Given the amount of detail Jack asked for, Tony was fairly certain he had been sharing the same information with Jack as with Kyle. In return, Kyle was always open to share with Tony.

"I'm not sure what you mean," Tony finally responded, unsure of what to say given the intensity of Jack's questioning.

"Well, our largest client reported this morning that our product is completely down. Then I got two calls from other clients telling me about the same issue. So you tell me—what's up?"

Tony felt himself backing up on his heels as Jack spoke to him. "I knew Mixly had reached out to Kyle, but I hadn't heard back from him yet. And I didn't realize it was affecting others. I'll follow up with Kyle when he gets in."

"How have you not done that already? Why are you not connected with your team enough to know what the issues are? Do they not trust you enough to tell you when something has gone wrong?"

Tony stood there, taking in the rapid firing of questions. He paused, not sure how to respond. Realizing he needed to say something, he managed to reply, "I'll get right on it."

He turned and looked at his phone. Still no response from Kyle. He went to find Molly and the team, trying to shake off Jack's questions that were now repeating inside his head.

"Maybe he's right. Maybe I don't know the team," Tony said to himself. "Wouldn't they have said something to me? Wouldn't Kyle have reached out? Maybe they don't trust me. Maybe I don't know what I'm doing."

A vibration from his phone interrupted the talk.

Are you here? Robert's text asked. *Need to talk.*

Meet u at ur desk. Tony replied.

Tony walked over to the team's area. Shaking off his thoughts, he ran through his mental checklist of all the possible areas that could be causing issues with the product.

"I just got done talking to Jack," Tony said to Robert.

"We don't have time for that. I need to show you something," he said.

"It's about the new product, isn't it?"

"How did you know?" Molly asked as she approached the two. "We've only started receiving help tickets in the last ten minutes."

"Tickets? Just now?" Tony was confused. "I just heard from Jack about the three clients from earlier this morning."

"Only three? Well then, I'll stop worrying about the fifty other tickets that have just come in," Robert said, trying to ease the tension they were all feeling.

Tony tried to laugh, but couldn't even fake it. Instead, he went right into what he knew about the situation, which wasn't much. Tony shared the feedback he received from Jack, without the editorial comments. Robert helped fill in the gaps based on what he had seen this morning. The help tickets were all the same. Customers were experiencing significant outages in the software Gr8Lyf serviced. They relied on the product to complete their day-to-day transactions with their own customers. The tickets showed that the product wasn't responding, meaning customers weren't getting the information they needed—meaning they weren't getting paid. Tony got more and more tense as they continued to dig into the issue.

"The strange thing is," Robert said, "that the tickets are coming in almost the order of when the customer bought the product."

"Which is why we heard from Mixly so quickly," Tony said, thinking out loud.

"And why Jack was involved," Robert muttered.

Tony shared the theories that were beginning to bounce around in his head. The three debated for some time, knowing that although time was critical, they didn't want to go down a rabbit hole in pursuit of the wrong issue.

"Yeah, for sure. Are you sure that's the problem?" Molly asked.

"I'm not, but I don't have much more information to go on. Do you?" Tony asked, unsure of his decision.

"Fair," Robert said, nodding. He enjoyed these types of issues and had been through similar exercises in his own start-up. He shook his hands as if warming up to play a piano.

"I'm on it. Give me thirty minutes."

Tony went back to his desk and sat down, exhausted. He put in his earbuds to help him focus and regain his composure. He turned on his computer and sent a couple of IMs to Molly as he reviewed the tickets that had come in. But his mind kept wandering back to the words Jack had used. The feeling that he had let him down. That he had somehow let the team down.

"I can't believe I could let this happen. You knew this job would be too much. Yet you jumped into it anyway," he said to himself.

Robert put his hand on Tony's shoulder. "Am I interrupting something?"

"Huh?" asked Tony.

Robert pointed at Tony's blank computer screen; it was in sleep mode.

"I found the issue. You were right. Well, your second idea was right. But you were still right."

BAND-AID

Tony rolled his desk over to Robert's so they could sit side by side. Molly joined them with her laptop. The rest of the team were at their computers, eating at their desks. It was lunchtime, but nobody was going anywhere given the situation.

Tony leaned over to get a better look at Robert's multiple screens. Tony pictured this was what it would be like to be a day trader, constantly looking at different metrics, numbers, and other statistics to monitor the hour-by-hour fluctuations. Only instead of stocks, Robert was monitoring the utilization of the company's products. Normally green to signify all was performing well, the metrics highlighting the flailing product were red.

"If you look here, you can see what's going on."

Tony followed Robert's direction and explanation. "The end user won't recognize the issue because the system allows them to keep going in the process. At the same time, our customers aren't seeing the outage, so the customer thinks all is fine. They don't even realize there is an issue. So we had a lot of people going through the motions but not realizing that anything was wrong."

"I thought our fix over the summer resolved this."

"No. Unfortunately that fix hid the real issue even further. And it's only coming to the surface with those clients now as they use the product more."

Tony's heart sunk. He had pushed for that fix within the team. And throughout the company. Now it was becoming clear that it was just a poorly placed Band-Aid.

"So we released a product that didn't work?" Tony finally said.

"No. I mean yes," Robert said and then smiled. "Yes, the product didn't work. The bugs we've been battling were signs of the bigger issue. But because we didn't really know why, we kept battling the symptoms and not the problem. It's clear now what the problem is. I guess we needed to truly break the system to know what was wrong with it."

"That's just great," Tony said, sounding defeated and frustrated. "We're losing time for those who are experiencing the outage now, but also for the other clients who haven't been affected yet. We need to fix this for good. And quickly."

"That's what I'd like to know," said Jack from behind them. Up to that point, the office floor was as silent as a library. Jack's question felt like someone had dropped a large book, which created an echoing boom across the office.

He had his head down as he walked up, looking at his phone while he typed.

"I've got Mixly calmed down, but it wasn't easy. Tell me good news."

Robert repeated his explanation of what he had found. Jack put his phone away and started swaying as he listened. Tony interjected, describing the impact of the original intended fix.

"Why didn't this issue come up earlier?"

Tony started to describe his idea behind the original fix but was quickly cut short.

"That's not what I was asking," snapped Jack. He paused, recognizing that other team members were overhearing the conversation. "I need to know what we'll do to make sure this doesn't happen again. And I need to know by the end of the day."

"I will do that," Tony said softly.

As Jack walked away, Tony, Molly, and Robert took a collective breath before pulling the team together to create a plan.

OFF THE PEDESTAL

Over the course of the next week, the team hustled on their plan. They all put in countless hours to not only get customers back up and running, but to create a permanent fix. The bleeding had stopped, but not until nearly 80 percent of their clients had been affected.

During that week, Tony worked hard but remained distant from others around him. His meetings were short, uninformative, and lacked the collaboration of his earlier meetings. He came to meetings flustered and unprepared, which was uncharacteristic of the expectations he had established. Molly used to joke that he had an agenda prepared for every meeting, but she hadn't had a reason to make that joke recently. Without being prepared, Tony tended to focus on details that were either too low level for the group or completely irrelevant. Tony could sense the frustration within the team but chalked it up to the high levels of tension.

Morning stand-up meetings had ceased during this time as well. "The team knows what to do," Jack had said when questioned on his decision by the leadership team. Dave and Kyle pressed Jack on the need to stay connected at such a crucial time. Tony, on the other hand, was relieved to be able to hide behind his desk instead of having to show his face in front of everyone. He was happy to keep his earbuds in, even if he didn't turn them on.

However, today was the first morning to reinitiate the morning standup ritual. Tony walked into the office with only a few minutes to spare before the bell would go off.

"Where have you been?" Kyle asked as Tony neared his desk. "I've been trying to reach you for the last two days."

"I'm fine," Tony said quickly. The two hadn't talked much over the last week. Although both were obviously busy trying to get through customer complaints and system issues, Tony responded less timely and frequently to Kyle's requests for a call or even a meeting.

The horn sounded as Kyle was about to ask another question.

"We'd better go," Tony said slowly.

The two walked into the gathering room. Most of the other employees were in the room looking toward Jack, who was up on his chair kicking off the meeting. The normally lively group had a different feel this morning. The past week had taken its toll on everyone. People wore blank expressions, as if they were avoiding making any moves so as not to be seen. The team was tired from the long hours and frustration of the seemingly unending process.

Jack began the meeting in his typical fashion. The break from the meetings seemed to rejuvenate him. He was smiling, but his voice carried a tone that mirrored the frustration the rest of the team felt.

"Good morning, everyone. The last seven days have been a good reminder that we're at a point where we all need to stay focused. Some of us have learned this ability over the years with this company. But those of us who may be new, we may not have had a chance to experience this. Perhaps we are getting overconfident with recent wins and not carrying forward with what we need to do."

Tony could feel his body tensing up. Although Jack was talking to everyone, Tony felt like his comments were directed to nobody else but him.

Jack looked across the crowd of employees. "Now's not the time to lose focus," he repeated. "I want all of you to maintain the effort needed to finish this year as our best year ever. Kyle, tell us how we're doing."

"At last count, we're on pace for a record year. The new product has helped us get there, but—"

"Thank you, Kyle. This is a great example of what I mean by focus. We cannot lose sight of what's most important, which is taking care of our customer. While we are bringing in new sales, we can't let our long-time relationships slip. We are maturing as an organization and can't experience issues like this anymore. Agree?" he asked the group.

Tony felt like he was growing smaller with each second of silence, as if an imaginary spotlight was shrinking him bit by bit.

"Shouldn't we expect better out of ourselves?" Jack asked to fill the silence, but the question only resulted in more.

"I don't see how we can continue to expect to grow if we're not holding ourselves accountable for our work. Our clients deserve better, and we should expect better out of ourselves. Let's all move forward with the expectation that we'll do better."

Jack stepped off his chair and walked out of the room, leaving the others standing motionless. If anyone in the room was hoping to feel motivated again after a long week, Jack's quick exit confirmed that they had come to the wrong place. Finally, one by one, as if woken from a trance, colleagues started to move toward the door in silence.

Tony, on the other hand, remained still. He looked at others as they passed, but nobody returned his glance.

"Hey, are you OK?" a voice finally asked.

"Oh, hey, Kyle. It felt like I just had the rug pulled out from under me. I felt like Jack was talking directly to me."

Kyle paused. "I didn't get that. Besides, we all fall off," he said.

"Fall?" asked Tony.

"Off the pedestal. We've all been there before. We succeed and then we fall. You've joined the rest of us. Now you just need to climb back up."

Tony looked at Kyle while he was talking but was paying more attention to the conversation in his head. *You've failed. Again. You obviously can't do this. You can't even stand up for yourself. Why are you even here?*

SINKING IN

"Well, that didn't sound like a productive meeting." Kate was listening to Tony's recap of the morning standup. Exhausted from pulling the details out of him, she resigned herself to try to move on with the night.

"Well, he was right. I didn't follow through on some things that I said I would do." Tony was tired too. It had been a long day. His head hurt, his body ached. He wondered if he was coming down with something.

"I'm glad you can admit that and take ownership. But I thought you said he was talking to the entire group?"

"It felt like it was directed to me." Tony was replaying the meeting as well as the last week of interactions with Jack. It had been a tense week for sure, but even he was becoming unsure of the details. He resigned himself to replaying the events that had led up to the last week.

"Did you talk to Jack about how you felt?"

"No. I avoided him the rest of the day. I figured if he had more to say, he'd come to me." In fact, Tony was doing more than avoiding. His focus on the product fix had created enough activity during the week to avoid encounters with Jack or anyone else on the leadership team.

"You have to start standing up for yourself." Kate snapped him out of his daze.

"I've just never seen anyone respond that way before. I mean, I've made mistakes before. I've had people get upset, but this time it felt so personal."

"What does Kyle say?"

Tony paused. "I haven't talked with him much either."

"How can you do that?" Kate said, standing up to clear her plate from the table. She was growing frustrated. The week had been long for her too; she had lost a key employee, which meant she had to take on more than a typical day required.

"You've known him for years. I've never known you two to not talk."

"He's been disconnected at work. He's got a lot going on. I just don't want to bother him."

Kate was out of options. "You need to talk to somebody. You can't avoid everyone forever. What about Dave? Can you talk about this with him? You're always sharing something he's said in a meeting or somewhere."

"He's pretty busy." Tony was staring at his plate, slowly moving the remaining food around. He was signaling he was done with the topic, and Kate was more than happy to take the hint.

They both quickly cleaned up the meal, as neither of them enjoyed doing dishes. As they finished, Tony grabbed his backpack, went back to the table with his computer, and sat down.

"What are you doing?"

"I'm getting back on," he said, inserting his earbuds. "I need to get some things done tonight."

"Did you forget what tonight is? You said you'd go with me to my yoga class."

"Oh. Yeah." Tony was about to make an excuse, but the look Kate was giving him told him that the truth was written all over his face. "I forgot," he said as he sighed. "Do you mind if I go next time? I feel like I'm coming down with something anyway."

BURIED

"Buried" was a word that the news was using to describe the unusual amount of snowfall to hit the city, even in early February. Tony had started to use the word to describe the amount of work he had on his plate. He said the word in conversations with his team. With Kyle. With Kate. It was true; he was buried with work. The Big Fix, as it had been nicknamed by employees, was now months behind the firm. Since that time, the number of projects that had come through to his team had doubled. The added work had required him to hire five new employees over the last three months. But even with added resources, there appeared to be little relief for Tony.

Buried became a word that would also explain why he wasn't available for other things. Why he wasn't around. And why he would go weeks at a time without seeing Kate.

"If I just keep working hard, I'll get through this," he said to Kate over the phone. He was calling to cancel their now monthly date night. Making time for each other every week was too much, in his opinion, given everything that had to get done.

"I'll make it up to you," he said as she hung up on him. He shrugged. *She just doesn't get it. Doesn't she understand how busy I am?* he thought to himself.

Kyle, too, was tired of Tony's excuses about why he wasn't showing up for their runs; eventually he stopped texting in the morning to check Tony's status. Tony seemed to be avoiding him during the day as well. Even during some of their busiest assignments together, Tony would never have been so absent as he was now. The only interaction they seemed to have was during meetings of the leadership team or with all of the staff. But instead of his normal friendly self, Tony communicated in a very matter-of-fact manner, seeming almost robot-like to those around him.

And the amount of work he was buried under seemed to prevent him from doing work. Tony found it strange when people asked him for help on a project or issue. "Don't they know how much work I have to get done?" he would say. "I can't get to those things. I've got all this other work to do."

His team could see him working; it wasn't about effort. But they needed him to weigh in on key decision that weren't moving. Robert had been elected to talk to Tony.

"Yo, Tony." Robert approached using his best Italian accent.

"Hey," Tony said, staring at his computer.

"I'm good," Robert said. "Thanks for asking."

"Funny. What's up?" Tony responded without smiling. He continued to type on his keyboard.

"Soooo." Robert was looking up at the ceiling. The exposed concrete seemed to echo his voice. "We need to talk. I need to get with you on some roadblocks we're having with this project. Can you talk now?"

"I can't get to that now," Tony said without looking up.

"Got it. When can you get to it? We're at risk for falling behind on this project more than we already are."

"I said I'd get to it. Can't you see how buried I am?"

THE WALL

While Tony found it difficult to do much else than focus at his computer, he was willing to make time to hire for his open positions. Over the past two weeks, he had made three offers, with each candidate accepting quickly. Tony was able to put his stress aside during the interview process to make sure he sold the role and the company. In fact, he enjoyed the interviews. They allowed him to focus on others instead of thinking about the work that awaited him after the meetings.

Tony was in back-to-back interviews for most of the day. He had just finished his third conversation of the morning, which meant he was halfway through the day. Although he had had good conversations with each candidate, nobody had felt like the one. It was frustrating, given the quick start he had with the other positions. But as impatient as Tony was, he knew he needed to wait for the right person to fill the role.

As he was walking back from the front lobby, he gestured to Molly.

"So, what did you think?"

"Nope," Molly quickly responded.

"That was quick."

"He had no drive. And she hasn't had any real project experience. Don't you agree? And besides, we don't need another dude here. It feels like we're becoming a large frat house."

"We're smelling like one, that's for sure." Robert rubbed his face. He hadn't shaved all week and had gone without a shower the same amount of time. He was recording a new album and, as was typical during weeks of recording sessions, focused on little else.

"Maybe we Skype the remaining interviews?" Tony smiled.

"You know what? I'm actually going to miss out on the next two," Molly said sheepishly.

"Oh no. I really like having your opinion on these. I feel like we're so close to filling our spots," Tony said. "Robert, can you still join?"

Robert stared at Molly, and she returned his look.

"Is everything OK?" Tony asked.

"Oh. Yeah." Robert was looking at the floor now. "Jack asked to speak with us."

Jack? Tony thought to himself. *He barely comes into the office anymore.*

Turning to his colleagues, he said, "I didn't know. Is everything OK?"

"I guess." Robert hadn't looked up. "He just said we needed to talk."

"Well, could anyone else from the team step in? I know it's last minute and all."

"I think they have meetings with Jack this afternoon."

"Oh." Tony trailed off. At that moment, he felt something heavy weigh on him. That feeling started to become warm. Then hot. It started in his stomach and moved to his back and then up into his neck. He could feel his body tense up.

He took a breath and said he'd follow up with them both by the end of the day on the interviews. Forgetting to say good-bye, he walked back to his desk. As he walked, he felt as if others were watching him. Evaluating every step he took. He refused to look around, though, fearing that others would look away when he caught their glance. He kept his focus on the ground three feet in front of him.

He grabbed the armrest of his chair and slid in as if it were a life raft. He exhaled and leaned back, allowing himself to relax his tense muscles. He sat there for some time, hoping the chair would disappear with him in it. Realizing he wasn't disappearing, he resigned himself to think of reasons why Jack was talking with his team. Without him being involved. He created stories in his head, but that only increased his body temperature.

Why do you think he's talking with them? You know you're not leading the team. You shouldn't be here.

"You shouldn't be here," a voice called behind him.

Tony spun his chair around to see Dave standing there in his standard outfit of jeans and an untucked plaid shirt. *Even at his age, he could keep up with the rest of us,* Tony thought.

"You shouldn't be here. You have an interview waiting for you up front."

"You're right. Thank you. I lost track of time." Tony started fumbling through stacks of paperwork on his desk. Normally clean of anything other than a monitor and keyboard, his desk was becoming closer to a garbage pile. Days-old coffee cups, acting as makeshift paperweights, littered the small desk.

"Are you still free for lunch today? I'm looking forward to catching up."

"I'd love to, Dave, but I've got these interviews. I hate to cancel on you again. It's just a bad week for me."

"I can see that," Dave said as he watched Tony search through his desk. "If you're looking for her resume, it's on the floor next to your foot."

"Oh." Tony felt embarrassed. "Thanks," he said sheepishly.

"Don't mention it. Let me know when we can make a time work."

"Sure thing, Dave. Thanks again for understanding."

TRUE COLORS

Tony smiled as he walked back to his desk after his final interview of the day. The afternoon had been more productive than the morning. He had met with two great candidates back to back. Their energy and excitement about the roles had rubbed off on him. He was feeling light and almost giddy.

I need to c u. Tony read a text from Jack. He felt his energy quickly deplete.

Rather than text back, Tony headed straight to Jack's office. He kept looking at the two resumes to keep his spirits up, but the buzzing phone was offsetting those efforts.

Where r u? came another text from Jack.

I'm at your office. Tony texted back. It was true. He found Jack's office empty.

Roof.

Tony headed for the stairs. The roof had become an extension of the office. The area had a few lawn chairs, a table, a grill, and a putting green. In warmer weather, it was customary for the team to meet on the roof or hold casual happy hours there. In the winter, however, it was vacant except for Jack. He had developed a habit of enjoying a glass of bourbon as he knocked out some final calls and emails for the day.

Tony slowly opened the door to the roof, not sure what he would find waiting for him. He was pleasantly surprised to find Jack alone, both hands on his phone, staring at the screen while he typed. Despite the chill in the air, neither wore a heavy coat.

"Who were you talking to?" Jack greeted without looking up.

Tony had grown accustomed to not exchanging pleasantries with Jack in recent months. Jack had been out of the office most of the time for either personal travel or work. Despite the Big Fix, the new product had earned Gr8Lyf some excellent press opportunities, which Jack was none too shy to take advantage of. When Jack was in the office, Tony kept his conversations with him brief, based on the belief that Jack would ask for information if he was interested in what Tony was working on.

"I was finishing my last round of interviews," Tony said. "I had two great candidates who—"

"When do I meet with them?" Jack asked, cutting Tony off.

"I didn't realize you wanted to be involved. I can make sure you're included in the final interview process along with the rest of the team." Tony was trying to respond quickly to the conversation, as he felt like he had agitated Jack.

Jack looked up from his phone. "Why would you not think I wanted to be involved?"

Tony could feel the muscles in his arms and back tense, as if bracing for an impact. "I'm sorry. It's just when we last talked you said—"

Jack cut him off again, as if he were in the middle of a speech. "Are you that incompetent that you don't think the CEO should be involved with hiring people at this company?"

Tony opened his mouth to respond, but Jack continued. "I've been listening to your team. They are feeling lost, Tony. They are disorganized. They say they are confused. But somehow they are finding a way to get things done, even though they have no leadership."

Tony was confused about where the conversation was going. He hoped for more of an explanation. "I didn't know they felt that way. Can we talk more?"

"I think we've talked enough, Tony. Start showing me results, and then we'll talk."

UNCOMFORTABLY NUMB

Most of the office had cleared out. Not that 5:30 p.m. was late for others, but the tone and mood of Tony and Jack's conversation had traveled quickly down from the roof and into the office. Employees left with the hope that it would die off with nobody around. Instead, it moved around like a fog, trying to find whoever was left in the office. It didn't have to try hard. It found Tony ready to welcome it again.

Tony texted Kate, letting her know he wouldn't be able to stop by after work. He stared at the phone, waiting for her reply. She was never away from the phone and always responded, even if with nothing more than a simple "K." But nothing came.

"Oh great," Tony said as he slid his phone onto his desk. He started rubbing his neck. His entire body was sore after carrying around tension all day. His shoulders ached too, a reminder of the stress he felt.

"Didn't you get the memo?" asked Dave.

"Huh? Oh yeah," said a surprised Tony. "I mean, no. What do you mean?" He felt like he was coming out of a dream.

"Everyone has gone home. Didn't they tell you?" Dave said with a smile.

"Oh yeah. I'm just finishing up a few emails. How 'bout you?" Tony responded while going back to his computer.

"Jack asked me to meet with him for a few minutes. That was two hours ago," Dave said as he rolled a chair over and sat down facing Tony. He breathed a long and relaxed sigh.

"We were going through some new marketing pieces," Dave said, reading Tony's mind.

"Oh," said Tony, staring at his screen. "Is that it?"

"How was your day?" asked Dave, ignoring Tony's question.

"Fine," Tony said, nodding his head while staying focused on his computer.

"How so?" smiled Dave.

Tony looked at Dave from the corner of his eye. "I'm really just trying to finish up so I can head out."

"I see," said Dave. Tony wondered if Dave had a hearing problem or if he just wasn't taking Tony's hint.

Dave sat there smiling at him. After what felt like minutes of awkward silence, Tony exhaled and straightened himself in his chair. "All right. It was a tough day." He looked at Dave.

"Tell me why the day was tough," Dave said.

Tony paused again, struggling with the desire to explain how he really felt and wanting to put on a brave face. Perhaps it was the nagging pain in his neck that prompted his response.

"I feel numb, honestly. I've wasted the last couple of hours trying to figure out why. And I'm sitting here with you now, and I still can't tell you."

"That's fair. Let's start from the beginning then."

Tony stared at his screen again. Dave couldn't tell if he was thinking or ignoring him. Just as he was about to ask, Tony spoke.

"I'm pissed off," he said simply.

"OK. Why?"

"At what Jack said."

"OK. Why?"

Tony looked at Dave and paused with another long silence. "That he's right," he responded. "That I have let down the team. That I am incompetent."

"Is that true? From what I remember in our interview, you've had a pretty good run in some successful companies."

"He must be right. I've let down others before. Everywhere I've worked has been a disaster."

"How so?" Dave asked.

"I feel like this is therapy," said Tony, forcing a smile.

"If we had nicer couches, we could call it that, but we're stuck here. Next time I'll plan better," joked Dave. "But while it isn't therapy, I've seen this trend in people at all of the companies I've worked for. Whether they're young or have been working for a number of years, there is a pattern. Or at least I believe there is one. Do you remember our interview?"

"Which one? There were so many." Tony smiled.

"That's right," Dave said, laughing. "I think it was our second meeting. Do you remember one of the questions I asked you?"

Tony looked at the floor, as if his memory was laid out before him. Vaguely, he responded, "It was something about if there was ever a time I disappointed someone."

"Good memory. I asked you to tell me about a time when you felt you let someone down. Do you remember what you said?"

Tony stared blankly into Dave's eyes. "Do you remember?" he asked.

"You tell me first," replied Dave.

Thinking some more, Tony finally said, "I made up some bull about letting a customer down. Well, I didn't make it up, but I thought it was a pretty soft example."

"I know it was," said Dave. "What would you tell me today if I asked you that same question?"

Tony thought again and responded more openly than he could remember. "I wouldn't know where to start. I feel I've let so many people down."

"Pick one," said Dave.

"Remember the issue that came up right before the conference? If I would have caught the right issue—"

Dave cut him off. "That's great. I'm hearing you say that the issue was something that you did. Right?"

"Well, yes. Wasn't it?"

"You tell me."

Tony paused and said, "I guess I did catch it. I talked about my concern to Jack early on. We agreed to move ahead and take the risk. And we talked about it as a team, didn't we?"

"We did."

"And Robert and I had discussed it would be a top issue to watch."

"So why did you take the risk?"

"It seemed worth the risk to be able to get it to market in time. And I believed it would be a minor issue that we would eventually solve. And that's where I really missed the boat."

"Absolutely."

"Wait. What?" Tony was caught off guard. "I thought you were on my side."

"Am I not? I was agreeing with you that you miscalculated the issue. Wasn't that what you were trying to say?"

"Well, yes. But no. I guess I'm confused."

"Tony, many of us don't have a basic belief in ourselves," Dave said, gently smiling. "So without that belief, we doubt. We doubt everything, but especially ourselves. The way we talk to ourselves, and even to others, is shown in the words. Language becomes focused on not only what went wrong, but what we feel like we did wrong.

"When we make a mistake, we tend to overanalyze what we did or didn't do to cause that mistake. Because we doubt, we put the blame on ourselves. And we talk negatively about ourselves in a way that we wouldn't talk to anyone. Not even our worst enemy."

Tony smirked a little but was listening intently. He had forgotten he was still waiting for a text from Kate.

"And we repeat the process over and over," Dave said. "When something goes wrong, or we believe it went wrong—regardless of the issue—we continue to use the same damaging words, furthering our lack of belief in ourselves."

"But didn't I fail?"

"And aren't you human?" Dave responded quickly. "The mistake or failure isn't necessarily the main issue. It is this repeated damage of your belief in yourself. You're not really thinking of the failure, are you? You're thinking of yourself as a failure."

Tony paused but then shook his head, as if trying to shake off Dave's words. "But I think this is different. I've gotten myself in trouble so many times throughout my career. This isn't something new for me. I can show you where and when I've screwed up in each of my roles. I can think of one time when—"

"Well, that's interesting," Dave said. "You seem like you've had a good run in your career. Was that all luck?"

"Must have been," Tony said as he crossed his arms.

"And the references that we checked? Were they all liars?"

"I paid them off," Tony said, forcing a smile.

"Maybe. Or could it be your lack of belief in yourself? I cut you off earlier. You were going to tell me an example of when you screwed up."

Tony moved his arms to behind his head and slouched in his chair. "There was this time when we left out a key piece of one of the products we were updating. It delayed us for nearly three months. I felt like I was on an island from the rest of the team after that."

"Was this the same product that was the centerpiece of the business that you sold to your number one competitor? For a pretty good chunk of change, I believe. Yes?"

"Yes, but—"

"Do you see what I mean?" Dave said.

"Yes, but…" Tony stopped himself and thought about that example. "I've always focused on things that went wrong. Or what could have been done differently or better."

"And how others view you? Did they really put you on an island after that?"

"I see your point. I guess I didn't necessarily let anyone down, but it still feels like I could have done more."

"So did you learn anything from that experience?"

"I did now!' Tony laughed and then straightened up in his chair. "So how do I stop the cycle? I can't just all of a sudden believe in myself, can I?"

"Fair. There's definitely more to it than saying you're a believer. But it's getting late. You should get home."

"Oh man." Tony looked at his phone. "It is late. What happened to the time?" Tony started texting. Then he looked up. "Thank you for talking with me, Dave. I'm glad I didn't get the memo."

Dave laughed and stood up. He stretched his arms above his head.

"Before we go, can I ask you something?" Tony looked up at Dave.

"Anything," said Dave.

"If you knew my interview answer was bull at the time, why didn't you call me out in the interview?"

Dave smiled. "Why don't you think about that tonight, and we can talk again. Do you have time for lunch tomorrow?"

"I'll make the time," said Tony enthusiastically. "See you tomorrow!"

DOWNLOAD

"Are you OK?" asked Kate as Tony approached the table. She had been waiting in the bar for nearly an hour.

"I'm sorry. I lost track of time," apologized Tony.

"Don't worry about it," she mumbled as he sat down. She picked up her phone and started scrolling through emails.

Tony didn't catch that she was ignoring him and began to replay the day to her. He was talking so fast he was having trouble putting together a complete sentence. Even the waitress had a hard time keeping up with his order.

He went back and forth between his encounter with Jack and his conversation with Dave. Kate gave him a confused look but stayed silent. She usually had to pull information out of Tony, but tonight it was flowing. She only had to nod as he talked.

"Wait, what did you ask?" asked Kate, finally putting down her phone.

"I felt like I needed to know why they hired me. It's almost like he knew I was avoiding the question."

"Is it that, or is it something else?"

"What do you mean?"

"I mean, it was an interview."

"Yeah?"

"And interviews don't necessarily pull out deep information. You wouldn't expect someone to talk about their worst memory or issue. We don't lie, but we definitely don't show all of our cards to others."

"So why did he hire me?"

Kate smiled. "Maybe you're asking the wrong question."

"I'm not sure I understand."

"I'm saying that maybe you shouldn't ask why they hired you, but instead ask why you need to know why they hired you. Isn't it enough that they did?"

Tony looked down at the table. "But shouldn't I want to know why?"

"Absolutely, but you already know why they hired you."

"But…Dave mentioned that as well. That I'm not thinking about the good things I've done in the past or what I bring."

"You always do that. So if you know they hired you for the good things you've done, what are you looking for? Why are you asking the question? You got hired. You're there, Tony."

Tony looked back down and nodded. "I'm looking for approval," he said. "I'm looking for someone to affirm that I am good enough."

"Exactly. It's like you're trying to fill a void in yourself. If someone believes in you, then you'll believe in you."

"But why can't I do that?" Tony asked. "Don't people look to others to reaffirm their beliefs?"

"But you're not trying to reaffirm. You don't believe in yourself. You doubt yourself all the time. Yet, you're trying to find someone who does believe in you."

"So me asking why I got hired isn't the issue after all?"

"You've got it, Tony. The issue is that you need to recognize that you got hired and that you belong there. Does that make sense?"

"No. I mean yes. I think I get it. So now what?"

"Now I think we eat. Are you hungry?"

"I'm starving!"

LUNCH

Tony was looking at his phone, hoping it would help speed up time. The team meeting had run its course but was somehow still continuing.

There was a pause in the discussion, and Tony took the opportunity to ask, "Does anyone have anything to add?" He paused and looked around the room. Seeing no expressions, he said, "I'd say it's time to get back to our day. Thanks for the time, everyone!"

The team pushed away their chairs, some joining desks, while others walked back to their desks. Molly walked over to Tony.

"Are you OK? I've never seen anyone more excited to end a meeting," she joked.

"Was it that obvious? I'm sorry. It just felt like we were done."

"We are now," she laughed. "Good luck at your lunch."

"Huh?" asked Tony.

"Dave said he was having lunch with you today. Sounds like you two finally talked. Glad to hear it. Good luck!" She smiled.

Tony tilted his head as Molly walked away. He let his thought go and started collecting his things. He grabbed his phone and some pieces of paper, on which he wrote out some of his notes from the previous night, and headed to find Dave. As he turned around, he found himself nose to nose with Jack. It was the first time they had seen each other since the previous day on the roof. Both found it awkward to find words.

"Good morning," said Tony as he struggled to think of something else to say.

"I'd like you to document the progress on the team's projects and share it with me by the end of the day," Jack said coldly.

"Absolutely." Tony was happy that there were words coming out of his mouth at all.

The men walked away in opposite directions, Tony still on a mission to find Dave. He received a text.

I'm at the restaurant. Meet me here.

Tony walked outside, thinking about what he needed to put together for Jack. The cold air hit his face, waking him from his trance, and he turned his focus to his discussion with Dave.

He had so many questions to ask, about the idea of belief, but also about what he and Kate had discussed last night.

He walked into the restaurant and found Dave sitting in a corner booth. He had his glasses on, trying to read the menu.

"I really hate these things," Dave said. "They make me look old."

"Well, aren't you?" Tony grinned.

"Watch it, kid. You'll be wearing these things soon enough."

"What are you having?" the waitress asked.

Unlike the fast-paced vibe of the coffee shop next door, this Southern-themed restaurant offered a much slower pace, recalling a time when conversations were held over a kitchen table versus on the go. It was a welcome relief to the intense pressures of the office.

"The usual," Dave said.

The waitress smiled and nodded. "Should have known," she said, grabbing his menu off the table. "How about you, honey?"

Tony pointed to the special and handed the waitress his menu.

The restaurant was small, but packed in a good size crowd during a midweek lunch rush. The cramped quarters made for a cozy conversation between the two.

Wasting no time, Dave picked up where he had left off the night before. "So did you think about the question I asked you?"

"You meant the question I asked," Tony said.

"Yes, you're right," Dave replied.

"I talked with Kate last night. She was really helpful. She didn't give me an answer, but rather asked if I was asking the right question."

"Oh really," Dave said. "What question is that?"

"She asked why I was even asking the question. She wondered why I needed to seek approval when I already knew the answer."

"And what did you think about that?" he asked.

"I didn't understand at first, but the more I've thought about it, the more I think I understand. By asking why you decided to hire me, I'm seeking approval from you. And not just you, but from others."

"I knew Kate was a smart woman. Well done."

Tony continued, "What I don't understand is why that's wrong. Don't we seek approval from others all the time?"

"Good question. People do seek approval, but when we don't believe in ourselves, we seek it from others. We are in essence hoping to fill that void. But what happens is that by not believing in ourselves, we are never able to fill that gap. It becomes an endless hole we are trying to fill. So we go from person to person trying to find that approval."

Tony nodded. "I think I can buy that."

"And not only that," Dave continued, "but because we can't fill the void with people, we never truly gain the self-confidence we need. So we reinforce that we aren't good enough. Even when things are going well, we find opportunities to sabotage ourselves."

Dave unfolded his napkin and drew two arrows with large spaces in between them. In front of the first arrow on the left side of the page, he wrote the word "Approval."

APPROVAL →   →

"If belief is lacking, we're left trying to deal with specific situations or even day-to-day life without a vital part of us. Without that sense of belief, we have a void internally. So we find ways to fill this void to get through the difficulties of each day. And we do that in two very unique ways."

"How so?"

"First, we try to find approval from others around us. And typically it's not just one person. We may need to find it through multiple people. Close friends or even co-workers."

Tony looked down at the napkin. "What's the other way?"

"The other way," Dave continued, "is that we find ways to hold ourselves back. Without our own sense of belief, we maintain the status quo. We find ways to ensure we aren't good enough."

"How do you mean?" Tony asked, starting to play with his napkin.

"Take me back to when you discovered the product issue last fall."

Tony looked up at the ceiling as he thought back to the beginning of the issue. It had been some time since he had thought about that period, although he knew he had been carrying it with him.

"It wasn't a very good time," Tony said quickly, folding his arms across his chest. He wasn't feeling as open to sharing as he was last night.

"Think about it some more," Dave said. "What were some of the things you were saying to yourself back then?"

"I felt like I had created a mess. That I had caused the whole thing."

"Let's go back to what we talked about last night. Are you thinking of the real situation, or are you thinking about your perception?"

"I didn't help the situation, that's for sure," said Tony, slowly releasing the tension in his arms.

"So when I hear people say things like that, it typically means that they don't believe in themselves. That they don't believe they have the ability to be successful. In a way, you tried to fill that void with continued head trash."

"Head what?" Tony asked.

"Head trash is the negative thoughts we have about ourselves. The more trash we talk to ourselves, the more it keeps us from believing in ourselves."

"I guess I didn't realize I was doing that," Tony said, getting heavy in his chair.

"Who's hungry?" asked the waitress.

DIGGING IN

"Here's the salad," the waitress said, sliding the plate to Dave, "and here's the Heavenly Special." She passed Tony his plate, which included mashed potatoes and gravy between two large pieces of fried chicken. On top of this creation was a generous portion of cheese and bite-sized pieces of bacon.

Dave's eyes widened as looked at Tony's plate. "I don't think I've ever seen anyone order that before," he said as he navigated his salad.

"Very funny. It's too good to pass up here. Have you tried it?"

"Are you kidding me? I thought you avoided that stuff. You come off as the health guy," Dave said.

"It's OK to get some protein every now and then, right?"

"So, you were saying?" Dave said, trying to refocus the conversation.

"Yeah, right," said Tony. "I shouldn't say that I didn't know I was talking head trash. I know I don't always talk positively about myself, but isn't everyone critical of themselves?"

"Sometimes. But not everyone lets it impact their lives," Dave said.

"But didn't I mess up?"

"Don't we all make mistakes?" Dave quickly responded.

"Well, sure. But…" Tony paused.

"Everyone makes mistakes. At work. At home. On our way back and forth to work and home. Life happens. When we make a mistake, it's usually not the mistake we are focused on. Instead, we worry about how we are perceived by others. That influences how we feel about our mistake, and ultimately ourselves.

"What happened in last week's basketball game?"

"You mean the missed free throw?" Tony said. "I thought they were going to pull it out."

"Yes. Do you know what the player said at the end of the game? He said he let the team down. The missed free throw didn't come up, but rather how it affected his teammates."

"Isn't that normal?"

"Absolutely. But do you know what he also said? He said he's going to go back to the basics and go back to his process. He can go back to practice and do the things that will make him successful the next time.

"If he were truly focused on approval, he would be waiting for his punishment from the coach or his team. Very few mistakes actually deserve a punishment. You were waiting for your punishment, so you shut down and took it."

Tony felt like he had been woken out of a trance. "I didn't realize I had a choice in the matter."

"Of course you wouldn't have. How do you think that has affected the relationships with those around you?"

"Not well," Tony said quietly. He thought about the last time he spent any quality time with Kate. Or had a beer with Kyle. "I guess I didn't realize I was shutting down."

"And when we shut down, we only hear what's wrong with us rather than what's right. Whether that comes from us or someone else. How have your conversations been going with Jack?"

"You've heard about those?" Tony said quietly. He put his fork down, somewhat embarrassed.

"If we don't have the approval, or belief, in ourselves, we look to others to fill that void."

"It feels good when he acknowledges the work I do. I guess I've felt like if he values my work, I need to take the punishment when I mess up."

"So you shut down again," Dave said. "When someone doesn't approve, it reinforces that lack of belief in yourself. And there we begin to lose control of ourselves."

"How do you mean?" Tony asked.

Dave pulled out the napkin and wrote "Control" in the next open spot.

APPROVAL → CONTROL →

"By not having belief in yourself or approval, it affects how you treat yourself and how you interact with others. You've in essence given up control of yourself. You start to allow other people or other things to lead your life. You lose focus on yourself and what matters to you. Take your lunch, for example."

"Hey, there's nothing wrong with trying new things," Tony said crossly.

Dave was about to respond when the waitress approached. She looked back and forth between the two. "I can just leave this here," she said as she placed the check on the table and quickly backed away.

"Tony, all I'm saying is that it's important to think about how you've changed during the time you've been working here, and especially since before the scene of the crime."

"The scene of the crime?" Tony asked. "Is this something you've made up?" He began to pick at his food.

"Tony, I'm…" Dave stopped. His phone had beeped, reminding him of the time and that he was late for his next meeting. "Oh no. Tony, I'm sorry. I need to bolt. I'll pay for this on my way out. Can we talk again tomorrow?"

Tony continued to push his uneaten food around with his fork. He finally muttered an "OK" but continued to stare at his plate. The cheese hung off the plate and onto the table.

Dave walked out of the restaurant, leaving Tony to stare at his meal alone.

LOOKING IN THE MIRROR

Tony walked into his apartment and slowly closed the door. He was still feeling the weight of the lunch. He had walked away from his plate without eating another bite, but he kept chewing on what Dave had said during their time together. He felt angry about what Dave said. Confused that he might have been right. He was hardly able to concentrate on much else.

The doorbell rang.

"Hi!" yelled an excited Kate from the other side.

"Oh crap," whispered Tony. He knew he had forgotten something. They were planning to celebrate her promotion tonight by going out for dinner. It was the first time they were going somewhere nice in quite a while.

"How are you?" asked Kate, walking in.

"Fine," Tony said quickly.

"Don't you need to get ready?" asked Kate. Her tone dropped. She recognized that something was up.

"Of course. Give me five minutes?"

Tony went to his bedroom to change his clothes. They had been talking about this night for the last week. The promotion was the main reason for dinner, but it also was a chance to reconnect, in Kate's words. The months since the holidays had been busy. Kate's work demands were increasing, hence the promotion. But she had also added another yoga studio class. When they did have time to go out, it was either with friends or for a work-related purpose. Both were coming off busy times, and this was a night just for them.

How could you forget about this night? Did you at least get a card?

He hadn't.

Tony added a few extra layers of deodorant, hoping that would wake him up. Even though this brand of deodorant promised confidence, he wasn't feeling it, no matter how much he applied.

Resigning himself to his condition, he gave one last look in the mirror. He checked his hair, flicking some pieces back into place. He looked at his face and rubbed his newly grown beard. Normally clean shaven, he chalked the facial hair up to being a popular look, even though he had no interest in the latest trends.

He continued to stare at his reflection in the mirror, looking for anything he may have missed. He started noticing things he hadn't before. He looked straight into his eyes. They looked tired, with red bags underneath to support his assessment.

Noticing he was hunched over, he straightened himself up. He usually prided himself on his better-than-average posture. His mother had undergone back surgery after a bad car accident when he was younger. He knew the pain that came with having a bad back and recognized a similar hunch that his mother had worn leading up to the surgery. As he moved his back around, he slid his hands from his hips to his stomach and gave the softness he was feeling three slow pats. He exercised regularly, or he had until the last few months. Or was it six months? The pats made him believe it was closer to six months.

Dave was right, and tonight was proving it. He had forgotten about the night he and Kate had planned. He thought about his past conversations with Kate and how they hadn't been the same. He thought about his interactions with his team and cringed. He realized he was losing control in so many ways.

"Oh crap," Tony said aloud without realizing it.

"Is everything OK? We're going to be late if we don't hurry," Kate scolded.

"No. I mean, yes. I mean…" He turned off the bathroom light and went to find Kate.

"We need to go," Kate snapped.

"I've been a jerk," Tony said. "I completely forgot about tonight. You have every right to be pissed at me. I'm sorry."

Kate knew he had forgotten but was thrown off by his response. She slowly found her words and looked at him.

"You're right." Smiling at him, she said, "Can we go though? It sounds like we have a lot to talk about."

STARTING DOWN THE PATH

Tony was walking briskly to work, partly to keep himself warm. The unusual cold this late in winter was surprising to all in Nashville. His fast pace was also to make sure he found Dave. He desperately wanted to share what he had come up with in the week since their last lunch.

As he entered the building, he saw Dave walking out of the elevator. Dave typically traveled light. What little technology he used was simple and sleek. The box he was holding in both hands almost disguised him.

"Dave?"

"Hey, Tony. Hey, I've been meaning to reach out. But now's not such a great time."

"That's OK. I wanted to talk with you about our lunch last week. I'm— Wait, what is all this stuff, anyway?" Tony said as he peered in the box. It was filled with small hand clappers and other branded gag items you'd find at a dollar store, except these had the Gr8Lyf logo.

"We're sponsoring another event across town. Lori called in sick, so I offered to deliver. But I need to be there soon and— Hey, any chance you have a free hand and an hour to spare?"

"Absolutely. Where are we headed?"

"Here." Dave handed over the box he was carrying. "Follow me."

Tony and Dave walked out of the building pushing carts loaded with boxes and headed toward the ride Dave had scheduled.

"That one right there," Dave directed, pointing to a gray minivan.

They greeted the driver, Kara, and loaded the boxes into the back of the minivan. She was a thirty-something mother of four, judging from the number of car seats in the vehicle.

"You're a woman on the move," said Dave as he surveyed the booster seats.

"You can move those into the back row. We won't need them; this is my me time."

"Seems like an interesting way to spend some time for you," Dave said as he buckled his seatbelt.

"I love connecting with other people. With four kids, it's tough to get enough adult conversation. This allows me to meet all the people I want to before heading back to the grind," she said.

"Pretty smart," Dave said. "Are you sure you can get us there in time?"

"Don't worry, old man. I'll get you there." With that, the minivan accelerated through a light as it was turning red.

"Safely?" Dave said, smiling.

"You didn't say that," she laughed.

Tony looked out the window to see other drivers giving bewildered looks at the minivan speeding by. He gripped the seat tightly.

"So now," said Dave, turning to Tony. "You were in the middle of apologizing."

"I was? I thought you were apologizing."

"Sounds like we had the same thoughts, so I'll go first. I shouldn't have pushed last week. I wasn't trying to poke fun but was trying to help you see something. Sometimes my foot goes in my mouth."

"You were right, though. I didn't see it at the time, but I eventually got there. I shouldn't have pouted. You were only trying to help." Tony stretched out his hand, and the two shook.

"So good! Thank you. Now, you said you got there. Tell me what happened."

Tony went through the events of the last week—forgetting to celebrate Kate's promotion, seeing himself in the mirror for what felt like the first time. He even talked through some of the feedback Kate gave him.

"I was amazed by what she wasn't telling me over the last six months. I didn't realize she was feeling those things. But thinking back on it, I guess I really did know. I just didn't want to admit it."

"Admit what?"

"That I was changing and that I wasn't focusing on what was important. I don't know how some people can do it."

The minivan accelerated again, and the two saw the light turn from yellow to red as they went through the intersection.

"It was orange," said Kara as she looked in the rearview mirror, reading their minds.

"You're the boss," said Dave. "However, you get us there!" Turning back to Tony, he said, "Again, sounds like Kate is a wonderful woman. And I'm impressed you got to the final piece on your own."

"Final piece?"

"Yes." Dave pulled the napkin from the previous day out of his coat pocket.

It read:

APPROVAL → CONTROL → EMPATHY

"You discovered that by not having belief in yourself, you looked for that belief, or approval, from others. You gave up control of yourself. You stopped focusing on what was important to you, as well as the behaviors that made you successful."

"I see that now. But what does empathy have to do with it?"

"I'm glad you asked. As you found out last night by what Kate was saying, you've slowly been shutting down to being your true self, to being open with others. Kate saw this. And I'm sure others would say the same thing."

Tony breathed a heavy sigh. "You're right. I talked with Kate about my belief that others have been trying to knock me out of this, but I didn't want to hear it. The more they poked, whether Robert or Kyle, the more I shut them out."

Dave looked at Tony, waiting for him to continue.

"I felt like I was failing them. That I was a fraud." Tony put his head down and stared at his hands in his lap.

Kara looked back at them in the rearview mirror and nodded her head in understanding.

Dave allowed some silence for Tony to think before continuing. "You were insecure. Some people lash out when insecure. You, and countless others, choose to lash inward at yourself."

"Is that what Jack was doing?"

"Perhaps. Some people see issues and try to help. Others see someone struggling and unfortunately have other ways of pointing it out. In either case, if not corrected, you'll continue to spiral. Whether it's relationships with those who are close to you, performance at work, or our own health."

"How do I fix everything then?" Tony said, looking up again.

"You've already started down that path."

Tony looked confused. "I have? But—" Tony stopped as he was jerked forward, the seat belt bracing him as the car slammed to a stop.

"We're here!" Kara shouted.

BACK TO THE BEGINNING

"Do you have time to wait for us? This should only take a few minutes," Dave said to Kara.

"I'll give you twenty minutes, old man," she answered.

Dave smiled. "We'll see you soon!"

Dave and Tony entered the hotel lobby with their boxes to find the event was well under way. Various vendors had taken over the hallways with tables, large signs, and other marketing pieces. Countless sales reps stood by each table to promote their companies.

"I didn't know we were involved in an event," Tony said as he looked around. Then he realized who was sponsoring the event.

"We're not. But we're supporting our client. This is Mixly's annual conference," Dave said.

Tony could feel a knot forming in his stomach.

"Why didn't you tell me?" asked Tony.

"Tell you what?" Dave said. "I said I needed your help. You said yes. What else did I need to say?"

Mixly was another small technology company. They were similar in size to Gr8Lyf, but were well beyond their years of being a start-up. While most tech companies considered revenue growth a success, Mixly focused on its ability to create innovation from within that resulted in spin-offs of new companies. In the last six years, three companies had been successfully spun off, and two more were in the pipeline. Mixly's annual event was not necessarily focused on new products, but celebrated the innovation opportunities they believed all of their clients had. This year's event had a Vegas theme; each of the vendors had added their own twist to their table.

As Tony followed Dave down the hallway, he checked out the various Elvis costumes, blackjack tables, and even a kick line that had a well-choreographed routine.

"Mixly takes the themes seriously, don't you think?" Dave asked, noticing Tony scanning the room.

"You're telling me," Tony said, laughing. "Who came up with this idea anyway?"

"Wesley!" Dave shouted as they entered one of the larger ballrooms. He started waving to a small crowd gathered at the other end of the room.

Across the room, a young Elvis with a guitar and leather jacket was directing a small group of people. Elvis turned around as Dave shouted to him.

"Hey, buddy," Wesley shouted as he walked over to the two. "I didn't expect the big dog to make an appearance today."

"Nothing but the best for the King of Rock and Roll," Dave responded, extending his hand.

"You guessed my outfit? You're quick!" Wesley said. "Who's this with you?"

"Wesley, meet Tony. Tony, Wesley. Tony is in charge of our product development and customer service teams. He leads those who keep things running for you."

"No way. You guys are so great. I really appreciate all you do. Especially Robert. He was a huge help when we were having a hiccup just a few months ago."

"A hiccup? I'm surprised to hear you say that."

"Are you kidding me? You guys fixed it right away. I couldn't ask for more. Especially someone as small as me."

Tony felt relieved but also confused. For the last few months, Tony had agonized anytime someone brought up Mixly's name. And each time, he played through not only the events that occurred that day, but each painful interaction with Jack. Tony had wondered what it would be like to meet the team at Mixly. Because of Jack's reactions, he assumed they would at best be upset. At worst, he imagined them holding dart tournaments with his face as the target. Perhaps a piñata shaped as his face. Regardless of the vehemence he imagined, he always envisioned much more yelling than he was receiving right now. And no gratitude.

Wesley noticed the conflict and continued.

"Don't let one mistake get you down, man. It happens to all of us. What's important is that you made it right and learned from it. At the end of the day, you can't take anything personally. I know some people do, and that's unfortunate." Wesley paused and looked at Dave for a moment. Dave returned the look with a kind smile.

Wesley looked back at Tony and said, "If you believe in yourself, you can take everything that comes your way—whether mistakes, critical feedback, or even unproductive feedback—as a lesson. Take it for what it is. And then move the hell on. I hope nothing came across as too personal."

"None at all," Dave replied. "We were just happy we could help."

"That's great advice, Wesley. It sounds very familiar," said Tony, who was looking at Dave now.

"Hey, what can I say? I'm a slow learner myself. But I eventually catch on."

"You've come around for sure," acknowledged Dave.

"Rock on," nodded Wesley. "Hey, do you guys want to hear my Elvis impression?"

"We'd love to, but we've got a car waiting for us. This one might just leave us behind." Dave started nudging Tony toward the exit.

"Your loss." Wesley shrugged. "Tony, it was great meeting you. Dave, good to see you. Thanks again, guys."

Dave and Tony waved a final time and headed back to the lobby. They walked in silence through the busy hallway. Rather than looking at the entertainment around them, Tony had his eyes on Dave.

"You and Wesley seem very close," Tony said, as if digging for information.

"Yep," Dave said. "We've known each other for a number of years now."

Tony only smiled, allowing his silence to be a question. Dave acknowledged as much as he continued. "We worked together during our earlier corporate gigs. He led marketing, while I led sales. We did some great stuff together there and then when he started his first company."

"He said some familiar things, things that I've been hearing a lot lately."

Dave chuckled. "That corporate gig eventually had some rough patches. Some could be blamed on the market. Others were on us. It hit Wesley pretty hard. He and I worked together closely enough that I was able to see what he was doing to himself, so I reached out."

"Seems like you helped a lot," said Tony. "I would have never thought that someone as successful as him would have some of the same issues that I have."

"It happens to more people than you would think. Now, where is she? You don't think she left, do you?"

The two scanned for the gray minivan, knowing there was a solid chance they wouldn't find it.

Then from behind them, they heard the sound of squealing brakes followed by a loud HONK!

The driver's head appeared out of the window. "Where were you guys? I've been looking all over for you," Kara nagged in her best mom voice. "I had just about given up. Can we go now?"

The two men shook their heads and climbed into the vehicle. They grabbed their seat belts tightly as the minivan sped off as quickly as it had arrived.

STARTING FRESH

"So how did he do it?" asked Tony.

"It's interesting. In the same way that we close ourselves down…" Dave said as he searched for the napkin. "Here it is." He pulled it out of his coat pocket and drew an arrow from Empathy to Control.

APPROVAL → CONTROL ↔ EMPATHY

"When we talk about empathy, it is typically focused externally. Being able to understand or feel what it's like to be in someone else's shoes. Sound familiar?"

Tony nodded, still clutching his seat belt.

"People strong in empathy are not only able to pay attention to how others feel, but they can show concern and compassion. But to truly understand and show compassion to others, we have to be able to have those same feelings and concerns for ourselves. If we can't be kind to ourselves, how will we truly be kind to others?"

Tony had stopped nodding.

"So by empathizing internally, we open ourselves up. By strengthening our ability to empathize both internally and externally, we can then take control of ourselves and our actions."

"What do you mean, open myself up? Do I just start sharing my feelings to everyone?"

Dave laughed. "Definitely not. By focusing on empathy, I mean that you are able to confront events and actions of the past. That you really listen to yourself and the discomfort you have from those experiences. The physical pain you experience. You are able to understand yourself and forgive yourself for any mistakes, failures, or things that just didn't go your way. To create this empathy for yourself and others, you have to do three things.

"First, you need to acknowledge the event or events that are causing you pain."

"All of them?" Tony blurted.

"No, not all. Only the important ones. You don't need to dredge through everything in your life, just those that still cause you pain. Those that still create anxiety for you. What things come to mind when you go back to the beginning of those situations? What would you do differently? What mistakes did you make?"

"But what if they weren't all my fault?" Tony said.

"It doesn't matter," said Dave. Recognizing Tony's frustration, he lowered his voice and said, "Whether you were 100 percent involved or just 10 percent, you were involved in that event, were you not?"

"Yes, but..."

"Tony, think about it. By empathizing, you're trying to understand and put yourself back in your own shoes. So you need to accept that you were involved and that there were things you probably could have done better. It doesn't make you a bad person. It just means that it happened as part of your journey. That it is something you can learn from. You can't control how others responded during that time or what they said. You only can control you."

Tony was nodding again. "I get it. I see your point."

"But also, depending on the impact of the event, you may need to treat it like a posttraumatic event. You need to recognize that some events can leave deeper wounds than others. When that is the case, we have to allow ourselves the time to process those and to grieve. I see too many people go through an event and try to move on without processing it fully. Without truly understanding it. Without truly empathizing with themselves. Eventually, they leave or get fired from that job. Then they quickly find another job, only to continue to deal with the same issues that occurred in the past. They don't empathize. They don't take back control. And thus, they never approve of and believe in themselves."

Tony was quiet.

"What are you thinking?"

"I'm thinking back to my first job. Kyle and I had some great wins, but there was one event that happened at the end. I've always felt like I've pushed that down."

"I'm sure you have. How soon did you leave that job after that event?"

"It was pretty quick. I'm glad I left, of course. But I carried some of those feelings into my next job. And even to this one."

"Why do you think that?"

"I was hesitant to pull the trigger on a couple of early projects. I was worried about making a similar mistake, so I slowed down. I chalked it up to maturity or even having a better decision-making process, but really, I was afraid of repeating myself."

Dave nodded. "That's good to realize. Some people allow those failures to affect how they respond or even interact with other people. By not addressing the event, you end up with some very big emotional scars that can stay with you forever."

"Huh," said Tony as he thought about that last idea.

"The second piece," Dave continued, "is that piece of forgiving yourself and others for the event."

"How do you mean?"

"Take Wesley, for example. He started from the beginning. When things got bad, he decided to go back to the scene of the crime and talk through the issue."

Tony stared at Dave.

"By scene of the crime, I mean the event that caused the deepest pain for him. He went back to the customer that had the issue and talked it through."

"What did he talk about?"

"Well, for one, he apologized. But that's his style. Many people don't like it. I almost view it as a lost art. I believe we all need to be comfortable apologizing to some degree. Not for everything, but for those events that matter."

"Why?"

"By doing so, we show that we understand and care for the person. It creates the empathy needed to move forward.

"But before meeting with the client, Wesley also forgave himself. He came to peace about the event. By doing that, he was able to take any feedback he received as an opportunity to learn. It further strengthened the empathy he showed for himself. You, in a way, started down that path today with Wesley."

"Really? But we didn't talk much."

"Absolutely. You would need to have a deeper conversation with him to get at what I'm saying. But you've opened the door to have that conversation."

"I wouldn't even know what to say," Tony said, looking out the window. He could see they were getting close to their building.

"Today was a chance meeting—not the best time to address the situation. If you had more time to prepare and to acknowledge the event that happened with Mixly, you would be able to ask questions that would allow you to better drill down on things you saw in the event and within yourself."

"I see what you mean."

"So the next time you have a conversation with Wesley, try approaching it with a focus of curiosity rather than of shame. You'll take the feedback as ways to improve rather than as additional noise."

"The next time?" Tony asked.

Dave smiled. "You said you didn't talk much with Wesley today, right?"

"Yeah, but…" Tony looked at Dave, expecting him to respond, but Dave simply stared back at him, smiling.

"Kid, just listen to the old man," Kara said. "You're going to need to talk with him. And from the sound of it, you have a lot of others you need to talk with, too."

Tony knew Kara and Dave were right. He had been creating a mental list of people as they were talking.

Tony settled in to the thought of the work that was in front of him. He stared out the window for some time.

"You're getting ahead of yourself," Dave said, interrupting Tony's trance. "First, take the time to process. The conversations won't matter until you truly acknowledge the event. When you feel like you're at that point, we can work together on the list of the people you want to talk to and by when."

"How will I know I'm there?"

"There's nothing magical about it. There's no time frame. But it really is about being able to talk comfortably about the event to yourself and others. You'll always feel discomfort in the situation, but you should be able to talk about it confidently and without blame to others."

The minivan came to its now familiar sudden stop, signaling the ride was over.

"We're here, guys. Before you go, you mentioned there was a third step? I heard two—acknowledge and forgive. What's the third?"

"Oh, thank you!" Dave said. "The third is to be grateful. Be grateful to others as they give you feedback. But also, be grateful for the event. For from that event will come great learnings and future opportunities."

"So true," Kara said. "As a parent, I can't tell you how many mistakes I made early on. As our family grew, I was thankful for those mistakes because I learned better ways with the younger kids. It helped me enjoy those times more with the entire family. I'm a better parent for it now."

"I'm sure you are," Dave said. "Tony, I'm leaving for the conference tonight and will be back in town early next week. Do you have enough to think about until I get back?"

"I sure do," Tony said, heavy with thought.

"Don't worry. These are tough steps to take, but they're necessary because they will help build the foundation to not only move through the process, but also to move forward in life."

GETTING TO WORK

During the next few days, Tony endured an emotional roller coaster as he tried to take Dave's advice to process the big events to heart. He forced himself back into situations that he had intentionally avoided for many months, and even years, as he tried to think through them. Tony's typical style was to go all in on anything he took on. Once he started, he would push through, head down. However, that approach wasn't going to work this time around. And as Dave had pointed out, it hadn't necessarily worked for him in the past.

As he recalled the events, they began to play in his mind like movies. They would begin as small clips, each playing an awkward or sometimes painful memory. Slowly, the scenes would morph into a full-length feature. Squirming and cringing in his seat, Tony was watching them all unfold again.

In just those first few days, he was surprised by how challenging it was to face such unpleasant memories. He knew he needed help from someone on the outside and called Kate frequently to talk through his thoughts and feelings. He didn't want to get stuck in his own head.

Kate's involvement didn't make the process any easier. But by verbalizing his reactions, Tony found that it reinforced the empathy he was trying to build within himself. He could spend hours inside his own head before he caught himself. But by making those thoughts come alive, he could cut that time in half. Not only would Kate stop unwanted thoughts, but he began to get better at recognizing them.

As each event sprung back to life, Tony would write them down. When he was home, he would pull up old emails and calendars, and even scrolled through his Evernote files he used during that time.

"I can't believe you save these," said Kate, looking over his shoulder.

"It's helpful to be able to go back to the thoughts I had during a meeting, or just while I was scribing."

Kate pointed at the screen. "What's that?" she asked. "Is that something? By the way, what exactly are we looking for?"

"I had a meeting with Jack that same day as the event. He said some things that really put me down. I wanted to go back to that to see what came from the meeting."

Kate handed the laptop to Tony. He flipped through the pages, then came to a stop.

"Huh," Tony said.

"What did you find?"

"Not what I was looking for. I made a note to follow up with Robert on the response. Jack received a nice compliment from Wesley, and he wanted to make sure it got back to him."

"Did you do it?"

"I don't think I did."

"Oh, babe. Perhaps the meeting was so bad that you were overwhelmed?"

"You would think so. But apparently not. We talked about some other tactical items, but nothing more than that."

"So where did those thoughts come from?"

"From me," Tony said. "I've been finding the same thing throughout. Sure, there are a couple of nasty emails that I wish I hadn't received. But I'm finding that each situation was only as bad as I was making it out to be at the time."

"But you don't deserve to be treated that way. Jack did say some really rough things."

"You're right, but plenty of people say dumb things all day. I just chose to listen to the bad stuff. I guess I didn't just listen—I dwelled on the bad stuff. I let their emotions become my own. And with that, I missed a lot of important things. Like recognizing a team member."

Kate stayed silent. She could see Tony working through issues he had needed to for some time.

"I'm realizing that the biggest mistakes weren't the actual mistakes. Rather, the mistakes allowed me to beat myself up for something that I could have quickly learned from and moved on."

Kate smiled. "Good for you, Tony. So where do you go from here."

"Dave suggested I have conversations with others involved. Robert's definitely on the list now."

"Who else?"

"Wesley for sure. Kyle, too, as I cut him off pretty quickly."

"Yeah, you did," Kate said.

"Thanks." Kate's affirmation made Tony feel defeated.

"I didn't mean anything by it. I just…"

"I know. I'm just realizing all of the work I need to do. You and I definitely need to talk."

"If it's over a good meal, you know I'm there," Kate said with a laugh. "And I can wait. I do think you're missing someone, however."

"Who?"

Kate stared back at Tony.

Tony thought through his list again but knew who she was referring to. He had been avoiding the name and the thought of the conversation for some time.

"I know. Jack and I need to talk. Can I save him for last? No matter what he said, I can't control it. I can only control how I respond. And I'm realizing through all of this that I didn't respond well."

"You did better than most. And you're pretty amazing for even saying that you'll talk to him."

"Maybe I'll talk with him," Tony said.

Kate laughed and then kissed him on his forehead. "I'm proud of you. But can we go for a run? The sun's out, and we've been sitting too long."

"Now that I'll agree to."

ASKING THE QUESTIONS

Tony was gulping his coffee as he waited in the coffee shop. He had a larger table to himself, but was surrounded by the usual busyness of the shop. He was anxiously tapping his foot on the floor and fingers on the table in rhythm to a song by a local band playing over the shop's speakers. The music was unusually loud this morning, which was helping him pass the time as well as taking his mind off of his nagging bladder, given the amount of coffee he had already consumed.

It had been nearly two weeks since his last meeting with Dave. Tony had counted down the days until they could meet again. During that time, he not only started down the path Dave had suggested but felt like he was taking positive steps, or at least moving in the right direction. Although he knew there was more work to be done, he recognized how much lighter he felt already.

Tony also realized that this was the first time he had really spent any significant amount of time focused on himself. He had attended plenty of conferences and trainings provided by his past employers. Personally, he worked out regularly and ate right. But putting in time for and having hard conversations about his own self-improvement was something for which he had never made time. In fact, he had avoided those conversations, believing that either he had more important things to do or how he was feeling was just part of the game. Tony smiled and shook his head as he thought about how backwards his views were and how thankful he was that he was making a change.

Tony heard the door to the cafe open and recognized a familiar face.

"Good morning!" Jack said.

"Hey Jack! How are you?" Tony replied, putting on his best poker face. Deep down he felt his heart drop. Tony was typically pretty careful to avoid Jack lately. He even went as far as surfing Jack's calendar to avoid the chance they might run into each other.

"What brings you here?" Jack asked while looking around the room.

"Meeting with Dave," Tony said awkwardly. "He's helping me with some things."

"He is definitely good at that," replied Jack as he continued to scan the shop. "I'm meeting with a prospect. If it goes well, who would be best to pull in from your team?"

"I'm not sure I understand."

Jack sighed. "I've talked with you enough about this process. I'm not sure what more you need from me."

Dave walked up. "Jack, good morning, sir. Has your big meeting shown up yet?"

"I'm surprisingly early. Can you believe that?"

Dave laughed. "There's a first time for everything. Would you like to join us?"

"I would. Tony and I were just discussing how to handle onboarding a potential client."

Dave looked at Tony for a response but found none. "I didn't realize Tony's team would be involved in onboarding. Didn't we decide the implementation team would remain involved and help with the handoff?"

"How does that help us speed up the sales process?" Jack asked.

Tony was beginning to sweat, unsure how to respond.

"You said you needed a group solely focused on just that—the ability to onboard new clients," Dave said. "That function doesn't fit in Tony's world. They're too busy developing and enhancing. It would get bogged down. Hence the implementation group."

"That's right. I do recall saying that. I'll just talk to Kyle about it. Good morning!" Jack shouted over the other two.

Jack got up and introduced himself to a young woman and then pointed to an empty table. Tony and Dave took a collective breath.

"What a way to start the morning. Need another cup of coffee?" asked Dave.

"Just one more," replied Tony.

Dave left for the counter. Tony sat there, trying to regroup. For as much progress as he felt he was making, he found himself still disappointed. Even small interactions, such as those with Jack, continued to have a paralyzing effect.

Why didn't you speak up? What were you waiting for? Tony thought to himself.

Dave stood above him waiting. "Well?"

"Sorry?"

"Do you take anything in it?"

"Huh? Oh. No. Black is fine," Tony said, trying to shake himself back into the present.

"I thought so," Dave said. "Are you OK?"

"I'm fine. How was the trip?"

Dave was holding his coffee with two hands. "It was fine," he replied, eyeing Tony over his mug.

"That's it? You said you had some big wins."

"You also said you were going to work on being more vulnerable. How about we start with you, OK?"

Tony laughed. "That's fair," he said as squirmed in his chair. He looked into his coffee mug, then back at Dave. "It's still hard for me at times. Especially when I interact with Jack. I felt frozen in how to respond to him just now."

"I can see that," Dave replied. "Seems like there might be something else?"

"And I'm disappointed, too. I worked really hard on what you told me the last time we talked. I've been processing it and.... Well, I guess I just thought that with all the work I've done I'd be better."

"Better?"

"Like I'd be fixed. Like these things wouldn't bother me."

"I understand. Remember, the events you're working through have been with you for many months and even years. You can't just flip a switch and expect it to be better in a matter of days. Don't think of this as trying to cross a finish line like in a race. If you do, you'll never get there."

"I was hoping that wasn't the case. I really just wanted to be done with this and move on."

"You can move on, but you have to think about it differently. Rather than thinking about this as something to check off, think of it as training or practice. Think about a swimmer. Every time they are in a pool, they are thinking about their technique. Perhaps it is with their arms or how they kick their legs. But they think about how to make or continue new habits constantly."

Tony nodded. "I get it."

"In a similar way, with every new encounter you have moving forward, think of each as a chance to develop or maintain a habit or skill. Don't look back to the past because those either weren't good habits or, if they were good, you can probably do something to be better. Again, swimmers who have their elbows come out of the water just right start thinking about how their hands and fingers enter the water. What you really should focus on is not so much getting back to the past, but rather creating new habits and behaviors that get you to a new future."

"OK. That's helpful to think about."

"Well, good. We got off track as to why we are here, so why don't you tell me what you've been working on. I've been thinking about you."

Tony leaned forward. The cafe was full now, and the coffee was flowing strong in everyone. The music was drowned out by conversations throughout the shop. Tony told Dave about what he had worked through over the last two weeks. He talked about how Kate had helped him. He talked about the progress he felt he had been making. Whether it was the coffee or the atmosphere, he was full of energy and expression. It was clear that the last two weeks had been full of progress.

"That's great, Tony. You mentioned a lot of people who you'd like to talk to. I think that's a great group. Have you started any of your conversations?"

"I made a list, but that was as far as I got. I know I need to talk with them, but I guess I'm not sure on what exactly I need to say."

"Well, what would you like to say?" Dave asked.

"I think the conversation would be different for each. For Robert, I feel like I didn't support him when he may have needed me. To Kyle, I closed down and shut him out. I lost a lot of his trust during that time. They're all different."

"Maybe. But there is also a common theme."

"Yeah, I screwed up," Tony said sarcastically.

Dave laughed. "Yes, but more importantly, you're also being vulnerable. You're opening up and admitting the mistakes you made. And you're talking with them with an empathic mind—putting yourself in their shoes so you can learn from what happened and begin new habits. So I would keep those three themes in mind when you talk to them."

"What were they again?"

"First, you need to come forward and apologize. You did that with yourself. Doing that with others is the easiest way to open up. As long as you mean it, of course."

"Does that apply to everyone?" Tony asked. "I mean, how do I apologize when I feel like the other person was such a…" Tony bit his lip. "Such a not nice person?"

"What did we talk about that you have control over?"

"You're right. I'm only responsible for me." Tony paused again. "Man, that one is going to be tough."

"That's why it'll be important to move quickly into learning what happened. When you know the issues ahead of time, you can stay focused on what you want feedback on and what you can do differently. I typically say that the last question you ask is just that: 'What is one thing I can do better in the future?'"

Tony opened his laptop and starting typing.

"And second, begin focusing on new habits. This is where you can focus on specific things that you both can do in the future. This is an action plan in a way. The specific things you need to do together."

"Got it. And I really need to talk to Jack?"

"You brought him up. You must feel that you do."

"Damn it. You're right."

"And don't forget the last piece to this. Be grateful. Be grateful to those who you talk to. You're reaching out to people you care about and who care about you. You need to recognize them. Being grateful will help you have these conversations."

"Absolutely."

"But also be grateful for the progress you've made. You're changing yourself for the better. Make sure you also recognize that in yourself. It will help you when you start doubting yourself."

"Like this morning?" Tony asked.

Dave nodded as he took the last drink of his coffee.

"And for what it's worth, don't wait too long to schedule these. Within the next two weeks is good. Maybe more if calendars are tough. But do it quickly so you keep the momentum going. And, similar to how you organize your day, start with the toughest conversation first."

Tony took a deep breath.

"You can do it, Tony." Dave leaned over to him. "I can see the work you've done and your desire to really change. You're ready for this."

CONTROL

"So how do you feel after talking with everyone?" Dave asked.

Three weeks had passed since their discussion at the cafe. Tony had his head in his hands, looking down at the table in Dave's office.

"I feel a lot," Tony said, exhaling. "I'm exhausted. Surprised. Relieved. Angry, in some ways. I still wonder if I had to be the one to apologize."

"That's very fair," Dave responded, rolling his chair from behind his desk to the side table where Tony was sitting. "You can think of yourself as the better person if it helps. But by apologizing, you were able to gather some new information that you didn't realize about the situations. And perhaps about yourself."

"That's true. Robert's talk helped me realize how much I went into my own shell. I didn't realize it at the time, but he pointed out how difficult it was for him to find me—let alone connect with me. And Kyle said similar things. In fact, a lot of what I heard was the same. As I was going through the event, I isolated myself from a lot of people. Well, everyone apparently."

Tony paused to spin his pencil on the table, listening to the soft scraping sound. "I thought I was doing it to protect myself. But I have a feeling you know what I was really doing," Tony said, looking at Dave.

Dave laughed. "I might have an idea. Although you may have thought you were doing it for your own protection, it was actually a sign of how we can give up control of ourselves."

"How so?"

"Think of it this way. Robert told you that while you were isolated most of the time, sometimes you came out of that isolation, that you were there for him. Right?"

"I guess so."

"There were times when you were looking out for Robert's best interest. You went to bat for him, right?"

"Sure."

"But when it was you who needed the help, did you step up for you?"

Tony was silent. He hadn't realized he had a choice to stand up for himself after the event.

"Why didn't you go to bat for yourself? When things got tough, why didn't you stand up for you?"

Tony looked down. "I hadn't thought of it that way."

Dave drew his diagram on a piece of paper, drawing an arrow from Control to Approval.

APPROVAL <—> CONTROL <—> EMPATHY

"You've started to be empathic with others and, more importantly, with yourself. By acknowledging the mistakes that were made and giving yourself permission to forgive, you're now ready to focus on you."

"Me?" Tony said.

"Yes. To be selfish for yourself."

"That seems to be the opposite of what you just asked me to do. Why did I open myself up if I'm closing myself back down?"

"Think about what you realized just now. You've been ignoring yourself. As things got tough, you went into hiding. You hid from others, but also from who you are as a person."

"You mean how I've treated others."

"Yes. But also how you've treated yourself. Think about it. When you first started here a year ago, you were physically active. You and Kate talked about hiking together in the fall. You and Kyle ran together. Has any of that happened lately?"

"No. I can't even remember the last time I went for a run."

"What's holding you back?"

"I just feel so busy. I guess I don't know where to fit it in or even start."

"The most important thing to realize is that you've had to start at some point in your past. Whether it be running, dating, or even a new job. Remember that you've been there before. But it's also important to remember that you've just been through something, something that had a big impact on you. So it's worth looking at things differently. To bring a new approach."

"I have a feeling you have something in mind."

"You're getting good at this. The easiest and most effective thing I've seen others do to start being selfish is to set goals. To do that, I suggest "I will" statements. It's an easy way to refocus on the things that define us and are most important to getting us back to that spot. Let's use your running as an example."

"OK."

Dave got up and went to his clear board on the wall. The glass ran from the ceiling to the floor, and Dave was known to use every inch of space. But today it was blank. He started by writing "Runner" on the board.

"So you're a runner, but I like to use adjectives to define this better. What kind of runner would you say you are?"

"Do you mean like good or fast?"

"I'm the last one to talk about the best way to gauge running," Dave said, rubbing his belly. "It could be fast or good, but it should be something that defines what it means to you."

"I used to be a consistent runner, but man, I'm far from that now."

"That works. Let's use it. Let's write that down."

On the left side of board, Dave wrote: "I will run consistently."

"On the right side, we list the things that define that statement. These are the things that you need to do, or start doing, to get you there. So what does consistently mean to you?"

"It means that I run four days a week."

"And?"

"I would run with Kyle once a week."

"Anything else?"

"I'd like to get back to running one long run per week."

"What does a long run mean? Isn't running long enough?"

Tony laughed. "For me, it means ten miles or more."

"What? You really run that far?"

Tony laughed again.

"Let's write those down on the right-hand side."

As Dave wrote, Tony asked, "Why am I writing these down? I know what I want to do. Can't I just do it?"

"You could. But by putting pen to paper, or in this case, marker to board, you're creating a contract of sorts. A contract to live by over the next three months."

"Why three months?"

"So you give yourself the time to develop new habits. But also so you can update your statements. Perhaps you not only want to be consistent, but you want to be strong. That may mean you have to develop a new routine or new habits. It's good to document your goals and revisit them on a regular basis."

"So you're telling me that setting goals is going to be an ongoing thing for me going forward?"

"Absolutely. Every three months. Creating your goals gives you purpose, especially in tough times. They keep you focused. And your goals give you the clarity on what's most important to you, whether it be running or another part of your life."

"But why three months?"

"There's no magic in that number. Some do a year, others a month. To me, three months allows you to set a large goal and make real moves to accomplish it without losing track of it. It's hard to accomplish much in a month anymore, and it's hard for anyone to remember what happened a year ago."

"I like that. What are some other areas I should be thinking of?"

"We've touched on the physical already. This is how we take care of ourselves. How we exercise, sleep, and fuel our bodies. Or in some cases, how we don't."

"I'm getting back into exercising, Dave." Tony laughed.

Dave smiled. "But you also need to think about the other areas that matter. Our ability to be mindful is as important or more important than the physical. This can include our spirituality, but most of all how we get ourselves to have the best mind-set possible every day."

"Do you mean meditation? I tried that for a while, but I never could stick with it."

"That's OK. Being mindful doesn't necessarily mean we meditate. Rather, it means we are able to focus our attention on the present moment. We are aware of our emotions. And we are able to accept those emotions, as well as ourselves, without judgment. You don't have to force something to be mindful, but rather create a goal that you'll actually follow through with. For some, this might mean meditation or thoughtful breathing."

"Great. What else?" Tony asked as Dave wrote on the board. He was getting excited about the idea of these new goals.

"While those two areas have a sense of internal focus, the remaining two areas are more rooted externally. Our connections with others matter significantly. At the end of the day, we need to surround ourselves with people who we feel connected with—either through love, friendship, support, or guidance. And these connections are not a one-way street. They should be with those who we can give to, not only receive from."

"Let me guess. That's the social part?" Tony asked.

Dave nodded. "I call it relationships. Within this category, it's important to think about the connections that are most meaningful to us. And those that we need to build relationships with or, in some cases, rebuild relationships with."

"I have a lot of work to do there, don't I?" Tony smiled.

"Yes, you do," responded Dave. His lack of smile reminded Tony about the conversations he still needed to have.

"And finally is what I call purpose. This category includes those things that create the most meaning and purpose in our lives. For some, it may include the categories we just talked about. But for most, it includes our careers, which can have the most surprising impact on us, as you've found out."

"That's for sure." Tony sighed. He was feeling less excited than when the conversation started.

"Most people either put too much effort or not enough effort into their career. By emphasizing too much, you run the risk of neglecting your health or harming your relationships with others. You see this when people sacrifice time with friends or family in order to focus on their work. Others may work long hours, giving up things like sleep or exercise."

"I get that now. But what do you mean about those who don't put enough effort into their career?"

"Some people don't focus enough on their careers. You might see this in people who work for larger bureaucratic organizations or those who might be lost in their job in a smaller company. Regardless of the company's size, many employees become frustrated over time, given how slowly things work or how much politics are involved. In some, this can lead to complacency or a sense of giving up. They still work hard and put in the time needed to do good work. But they start to give up on many of the other things that matter to them in their career.

"By writing down these goals," Dave continued, "you're creating your checklist to develop a better balance of control for yourself. I would focus on only one 'I will' statement per category. Remember, these are statements that you'll repeat to yourself over the next ninety days. You won't have time for more than four."

"I think I get it. I'm just having a hard time thinking of what to focus on for the career statement."

Dave reached for his phone. "I'm sorry," he said. "It's a text from Jack."

"Everything OK?"

"He's texting me that he just emailed me." Dave smiled.

Tony smiled back.

Dave was silent as he scrolled through his phone.

"What is it?" Tony finally asked.

"I think we may have some goals for the career category for you. Grab a picture of this and let's head back to Jack's office."

ALL TOGETHER NOW

Dave and Tony walked into Jack's office. The office, one of the few on the floor, was surprisingly isolated from the other main areas and for good reason; it had the best view. The city skyline just outside the windows made it feel like the buildings would be listening in on this conversation.

"Who are we waiting for?" Jack said in lieu of a more traditional greeting.

"This is your meeting. Or did I miss a memo?" Dave said.

"Right. Kyle should be joining us shortly."

Tony stared at Jack silently. He watched as Jack paced back and forth behind his desk and chair as if he were confined to that small area.

"Sorry I'm late," pushed out Kyle. He was out of breath.

"Where were you coming from?" Jack asked.

"Stairs. Elevator. Out. Again," panted Kyle as he bent over with his hands on his knees.

"Ridiculous. I'm going to text our new receptionist. What's her name?"

"Cassie. And she's far from new. She's on her third month here."

"Right, right," Jack said, still pacing.

"Hey, man," Kyle said to Tony as he got his breath back. "Thanks for making the time last week. It meant a lot. You sure we're still on for this week? I can't be stood up again. It'll make me look desperate."

"I'd hate to give you the wrong impression," Tony said.

"Do you two need a room?" asked Jack, looking down at his phone. "Or can we get down to business?"

"We'll just have to gaze into each other's eyes during this meeting," Kyle said with a laugh.

"Anyway," Jack started, ignoring Kyle. "I wanted to let you know that we're in. I've got us a meeting at Knew."

Kyle started to slow clap but realized quickly his time on stage had passed.

Jack turned his glance from Kyle back to the group. "This is one that we've been chasing for a number of years. We thought we had him, but word got out about our issues from last year."

Tony held his breath, waiting to hear what was next.

"But they've also heard that we've rebounded from that and are ready to give us another meeting. And in fact," Jack paused, "they want to meet next week."

Tony exhaled silently, straightening in his chair.

"What they're really excited about is our latest product. They could see it filling a huge need for what they're working on in the next quarter."

"The next quarter?" Kyle questioned. "I thought we were still months away from even being close to a pilot."

Jack began to speak but instead looked at Tony.

"Well, yes," Tony said slowly. He turned to Kyle. "We're months away from a full release. But," he paused, turning back to Jack, "depending on the full scope, that timeline might not be as tough to achieve."

"They would need all of it. You should know that. They're always wanting the biggest and the best."

Tony could feel himself starting to tighten up. But he caught Dave's encouraging glance and nod. Tony looked down and exhaled slowly.

"You're right. They do want the best. But let's try to put ourselves in their shoes on this."

Tony stood up, grabbed a marker, and began writing on the whiteboard. As he drew an outline of the product details, he found himself gaining confidence the more he talked. And his impromptu presentation was affirmed by nodding heads around the table. Except for one.

"I still don't think you're seeing this correctly," Jack said with his arms crossed. "You're missing some very obvious and critical areas."

Clutching the marker so as not to lose his poise, Tony calmly asked, "What areas do you feel I've missed?"

Jack looked at the board and then back at the group.

"I've never heard you silent, Jack," Dave said.

Tony could see Jack still hadn't bought in.

"We can create a great project for Knew," Tony said. "To do this, I will…" He turned to the board and wrote:

- Lead "daily shorts" with project team
- Provide weekly updates to leadership team re: our progress
- Position Robert to lead implementation meetings twice/week.

Jack looked back and forth between Tony and Dave in silence. He picked up his phone and said simply, “I’ll make the call to Knew.”

WELCOME BACK

Over the next two weeks, Tony continued to try on his new sense of control. He could feel the difference at work. He started by immediately connecting with his team to pull them in and get them excited about Knew.

Their team meetings went back to being focused and purposeful as they were when Tony first started. After some trial and error, Tony saw the group quickly find their groove. They found themselves not only quickly out of the gate, but also ahead of schedule. But that's not to say the group still didn't have some fun. Robert was the first to welcome the after-meeting drink outings, especially when Tony bought.

Tony started each meeting by going back to the statements that he made to Jack and the leadership team. By the third meeting in which he did this, the team stood up together, put their hands over their hearts, and repeated the statements in a monotone voice as if they were in an elementary school classroom reciting the Pledge of Allegiance.

As a result of the newfound unity, Tony found himself back in a more familiar role. He was recognizing others versus micromanaging. He was appreciating rather than showing disappointment.

Despite the tight deadline, Tony remained connected to the people who were close to him. He and Kate talked about the project and expectations and started scheduling time together that wouldn't be interrupted. Although Kate was unsure Tony would follow through, she was surprised at how dedicated Tony was to meeting to those commitments. She would have been even more surprised to know he had also found time to look at engagement rings.

"So you still haven't found one, or is it that you just haven't picked one?" asked Kyle, running in full stride as he tried to stay even with Tony.

"Probably a bit of both. I just want it to be perfect," Tony said.

"You'll be fine. It'll come from you. That will be what makes it perfect."

"True."

"I'm surprised you're having an issue deciding. You've been solid lately. Good to see you doubting yourself again."

"Didn't want to disappoint you."

"You could never do that." Kyle was breathing heavier now. "Other than engagement rings, is there anything else that is getting in your way?"

Tony was quiet. "Why do you ask?"

"No reason."

"There must be something. Just say it."

"Jack. You're just different with him. Well, you're different now. You and your team seem to be in a good spot. You and Kate seem even more solid than before. But it's like you're still stuck where you were a few months ago with Jack."

"That's totally fair. I'm feeling it too. I didn't realize it was coming out."

"It's not like you're completely dysfunctional, but it's a difference. Didn't you say that you talked with him as well?"

"I did. We had a great conversation. It's just…" Tony fell silent for a few strides. "I've realized how much his words hurt. Dave explained that because I doubted myself, I created a void, so I had to replace my belief with something. I think I was looking for other things to fill that void. And the things Jack said…."

"So when things went downhill, he only reaffirmed your belief," Kyle said. "Or really your non-belief in yourself."

"Exactly. I don't feel like I've totally recovered from that."

"Have you tried talking with him about that?"

"Not in that detail. It feels awkward."

"No, I hear you. You should give yourself some credit, though. You've been working awfully hard on yourself. Remember how far you've come. It's a long road. You're not striving for perfection. You're trying to keep learning. And improving."

"Thanks, man."

"But do you have to work so hard right now?" Kyle forced out. "Your newfound confidence is great and all, but some of us are still human."

"Sorry, man," Tony said as he eased his running pace. "It just feels so good to be back."

"It's good. To have. You back," Kyle panted in reply.

APPROVAL

"That was good advice," Dave said, sipping his coffee. "Good thing you've started running again."

"For sure," Tony said, quickly trying to bring Dave back to the topic at hand. The sun was starting to shine through the office windows. Tony had asked Dave to meet early, and he knew it was only a matter of time before the rest of the team started arriving for the day.

"But I don't know what to say. 'Hey, Jack. How are you? That's good. Hey. So, it's still weird between us. And I want to know what I can do to fix it'?"

"What's wrong with that?"

"I can't just say that." Tony paused for some time and then asked, "Can I?"

"You may want to have some things prepared about what you've seen. Examples of what you've done. Examples of what he's doing. What you're doing to fix your things. But otherwise, I think you've got the idea."

"Dave, I feel like you're blowing me off. I'm really struggling with this."

Dave sat back in his chair and smiled.

"What's that? What's that you're doing there?" Tony quickly said while pointing. "I'm getting tired of that look."

"It means that you need to remember that you've come a long way. And that you're at a much better place than where you were when we first started talking about this. Think back to that first lunch together."

"I do." Tony sat back in his chair and let out a big sigh. "I remember I didn't want to address the issue."

"And how did you respond to me just now? You're getting more comfortable and confident."

"I see what you're saying." Tony sighed. "I just told you how I felt."

"Yeah, you did." Dave laughed. "Because of the work you've done, you're not looking to anyone to verify your head trash. You're not looking for approval any longer. Or at least I don't hear you saying that."

"No. I just want us to be able to work together in a better way."

"Remember when we talked about the emotional void, and how since you didn't have belief in yourself, you would find other ways to fill it? You've been vulnerable with yourself and with others. You've regained control of your own life. Because of that, you don't need to fill that emotional void. You don't need anyone's approval. You can approve yourself."

"I hear you. So why do I still find it so awkward to have this conversation?"

"It can be difficult to be open with people, especially those where trust might have been lost. But you can't change that. You don't have control over that. But what you can do is look at yourself and decide."

"Decide what?" asked Tony.

"To look at this and ask what you can do differently or more of to work together."

"I guess so."

"If you continue to work together the same way you have in the past—"

"I can't do that anymore," Tony said, cutting him off.

"Good. So you're going to have the conversation?"

"And if I stay, you're telling me to just go for it. Right?"

"Only you can decide that. But I know I'd much rather be open about how I feel than continue to fret about it."

"So I just need to go for it."

"Go for what?" Jack asked.

Tony and Dave glanced at each other. As Dave began to respond, Tony was first to reply.

"I was just updating Dave on some of the dynamics of the team. How are you, Jack?" Tony said, exhaling as he finished his question.

"I'm good. Thanks for asking. And your team has been looking sharp lately."

"Thanks, Jack."

"I'm going to run, guys. Good to see you both," Jack said as he walked toward the lobby.

"Thanks, Dave," Tony said, running after Jack. "Hey, Jack. Can I buy you a cup of coffee tomorrow?" Tony blurted out. He knew if he didn't take advantage of this moment, he would only continue to postpone the discussion. “I want to follow up from our conversation last month and talk about how things are going. Are you available?”

“I’m not available,” Jack said as he looked at his phone. Pausing to look up at Tony, he added, “But I’d really like to have that conversation. How about after work instead?”

“Deal. Thanks, Jack.”

FINDING THE WORDS

Pacing in front of the bar, Tony was questioning himself on whether he needed to have this conversation at all. He followed the checkered tile down one side of the area and then back. He'd slowly step his right foot on each white square, his left foot on a black square.

How is this going to go? Do you know what you want to say? Why are you even here again? Tony thought.

Turning around to retrace his steps, he responded, "You need to be able to have a conversation. You can't continue to communicate in the same way you're doing today."

Jack's signature tardiness was only enabling Tony's internal conflict. His only salvation was in the notes he had written down on what he wanted to address with Jack. He pulled out the note in his pocket that listed the outcomes of the meeting.

"Jack has a better understanding of what I'm feeling, and I understand ways that I can improve in how I communicate. We both have clear next steps on better ways to communicate and ultimately work together," Tony muttered to himself.

Tony took a deep breath and exhaled as he put the note back in his pocket. The note, pristine and crisp when he arrived, was quickly becoming as worn as the route he was carving on the floor in the lounge.

"I didn't keep you waiting long, did I?" asked Jack.

"Not at all," Tony said, extending his hand. Jack returned the greeting. Tony looked into Jack's eyes and noticed a tiredness that he hadn't seen before.

"How are you?" asked Tony.

"Fine, I think," said Jack, sounding almost confused.

In the year Tony had worked with Jack and the two years they had gotten to know each other prior, Jack had never been fine. He had been great, marvelous, fantastic. Maybe good or solid. But never fine.

"Is this a bad time?" Tony asked, unsure of what may have happened in his day. He almost went for his phone to check for a message from Kyle, but he held back as Jack said, "I'm glad we're doing this, Tony. Thanks for making the suggestion. I had been wanting to do this after we last talked but wasn't sure how to go about it."

Tony almost laughed out loud but instead said, "That's funny. I've had some of those same thoughts. Let's grab a seat."

"Good idea." The two headed for an open table tucked toward the back. With the sun still out, enough light reached the far-off corner.

The two started by catching up. It had been some time since they had talked about anything other than work. The conversation between the two was friendly. As their drinks arrived, they reached the point in the conversation where it was time to address the reason for their meeting, but neither was sure of who should begin. Tony took the opportunity to start.

"I've been feeling that we've been making great progress since last year. But I also think I still have things I can work on."

"And me," added Jack. "You're not the only one who wants to improve."

Tony wished he could see his own reflection to see if his face showed how surprised he was. Luckily he was able to quickly recover.

"Thank you for that. It sounds like we both want the same things. It would be great if we could talk about what those are and how we can help each other work toward those things."

"Absolutely. I know you have a lot to work on."

Tony turned his head slightly. Jack took notice.

"Well, you do," said Jack, trying to explain his comment. "But so do I. I know that and have known that for a long time. I sometimes wonder if I should be in the role I'm in."

Tony didn't have to look in a mirror this time. He knew he wasn't hiding his surprise.

TWO'S COMPANY

"I'm surprised, Jack," Tony finally said.

"Really? I couldn't tell." Jack smiled.

"Sorry. It's just…you come off as so sure all the time. I can't remember when I've heard you doubt yourself."

"Dave and I have talked about this before," Jack said. "Just like he's been talking to you. It's difficult for me to be vulnerable with others. I grew up thinking that by being vulnerable, we're soft. I thought it meant we have to share our feelings. He's helped me see the benefit of being vulnerable with myself and with others."

Jack continued. "I don't doubt that I can create a great product or a new company. But I still doubt, too."

"How have you gotten past it before?"

Jack laughed. “Luckily, I haven’t had to. Something, or someone, comes along, and I’ve been able to get out. I’ve been able to sell or exit. But this time…” Jack looked into his drink.

“This time I want to see this through. I think we have something here. But at the same time, I’ve never been here before. I don’t know what it’s like to do some of the things that a CEO of a larger company should do. So from what Dave’s helped me with in the past, I’ve come to realize that when I get to the point where I’m unsure about myself, I start to sabotage things.”

“How do you mean?” Tony asked.

“When I doubt myself and my abilities, I start doing things that externalize my doubt. When things started going wrong, you took the brunt of that.”

“Well, I don’t think I helped the situation.”

“Maybe we were both in the same place then.” Jack smiled.

“Too bad we didn’t realize it until now.” Tony smiled back.

“That’s true. I used to think that by being open, you had to share your deepest emotions in the workplace. What I’ve realized, and unfortunately tend to forget, is that you have to be open about what you want and what you don’t want. What you know and what you don’t know. I didn’t hold true to that.”

Tony felt like he needed to say something in reply, but took Jack’s cue that it was OK to let the conversation sink in as he sipped his drink.

“So what do we do now?” Tony asked.

“First, I think we need to establish some basic ground rules for us. We’ve both shared and learned a lot. I think we can help each other not get into this same spot again.”

“I like that.”

"We also need to agree to ways we can confront each other, in a healthier way, if the other isn't following those basics. I know I struggle with this, so perhaps we can give each other some grace."

"Fair. And let's schedule another one of these meetings so we can stay connected at this level."

"Absolutely. I don't think we want to go too long in addressing issues, so staying connected outside of the day-to-day will be helpful. For me, for sure."

"Cheers to that." Tony raised his glass as the two finished what remained of their drinks.

"So," Jack said as he put down his glass, "we still need to talk about one thing."

"We do? What's that?"

"When are you going to ask Kate the big question?"

THE FINAL TOUCHES

In the two weeks since talking with Jack, Tony was finding his conversations with Jack weren't necessarily lighter. If anything, Jack was pushing Tony harder because of how close they were to rolling out the Knew project. As the timeline got tighter, Jack's intensity increased while his patience decreased. But this time, Tony felt that he better understood Jack, and himself. And his new comfort level showed.

"What did I say?" asked an accused Jack.

"Do you really want me to repeat it?"

"I just said that maybe you're in over your head and that I could do it better." Jack paused. "Oh. I see what you mean."

"I knew you would. Now what were you really trying to get at?"

The two men weren't trying to achieve best friend status, but they were connected in a different way than in the past. Tony kept things in perspective. Both were more open to feedback. They kept each other in check. They confronted each other. They were open with each other. And most importantly, they were functioning in a way that the rest of the team noticed.

As the days grew closer to the Knew presentation, the excitement throughout the company was palpable. As Jack and Tony worked together better, so did the rest of the team.

At the last standup before the team left for Knew, Jack stood in his usual spot—but this time as an observer. He was watching Kyle and Tony talk through the presentation with the entire team. With his arms crossed, Jack smiled as he realized how far he had come. As he thought about all the things he had done to get to this point, he caught Dave's glance; the look was a subtle reminder that he had had some help along the way.

Tony and Kyle finished by asking everyone who had participated in the project to come up to be recognized. As they called off names, Tony realized how much the entire staff was playing a role in this project. By the time they were done, they had recognized everyone at Gr8Lyf.

"And last, but certainly not least, Jack. Without Jack, we wouldn't be in this spot. And we wouldn't be in the great position we are today with Knew."

"Thanks, guys," Jack acknowledged. "I'm blown away by everyone's work on this effort. We have a great opportunity to go big here. But the thing I'm most excited about is what I've seen within this team over the last month. We truly have the best team. And if Knew can't see that, then they don't know anything!"

The group laughed.

"Now get back to work!" Jack smiled. "Don't you know we have other clients who are paying us to do work for them?"

THE PITCH

"You said that?"

"You look surprised." Tony said to Kate over his shoulder as he fumbled through a kitchen drawer.

"I am, in a way. Aren't you? I always picture you being the quiet and calm one in these meetings."

"Don't get me wrong. I was calm when I said that they didn't need us." Tony closed the drawer and patted his pockets.

"Are you looking for the wine opener? It's in the other drawer. So what did Jack do?"

"Thanks." He opened the drawer and pulled out the wine opener. "He was probably the most surprised. But to his credit, he stayed calm." Tony pulled the cork out of the wine bottle. Kate handed him two glasses.

"Kyle's reaction was the best. He just froze and stared at me for the longest time. He was stunned."

"I can imagine. What did the team at Knew say?"

"That was the interesting thing. After I said that, there was this long pause. And then you could see the meeting start to change. They started to open up to us. It became a conversation, like we were hoping for. It kind of helped them let down their guard. We were all able to relax and get down to business."

"And then they said yes? On the spot?"

"On the spot." Tony put his hand in his pocket. He seemed to be searching for something.

"Is everything OK? You seem weird tonight."

"Yes. I'm fine. They said they needed to move quickly and felt like we provided them with what they needed. They didn't see the point of having another meeting with us or another provider. They just said yes."

"Kyle said they said something else. They had never seen such a good leadership team?"

"That's right, that's right! They used the word 'connected.' They said they've seen plenty of start-ups created by friends who co-founded the business, but never one that seemed as connected as we were. Their CFO even admitted that they were working through some issues and wanted to know how we did it."

"Wow. Who could have believed it?"

"It's like we knew what we were doing this whole time." Tony smiled and raised his glass.

Kate raised hers and clinked it against Tony's.

"We have a lot to celebrate," Kate said. "You've come a long way over the last year."

Tony stared at Kate, looking her straight in the eyes. “We’ve come a long way. I couldn’t have done it without you. You know that, right?”

Kate laughed and straightened her posture. “You’re so serious. Why thank you, kind sir. What’s your deal tonight? Are you feeling OK?”

“I’m fine. But I really want to say how much you helped me and how thankful I am for you.”

“You’re sweet,” she said and kissed him on the cheek.

Tony kept staring and put his hand in his pocket again.

“Now you’re weird.” Kate shook her head and started to walk out of the kitchen.

“Wait!” Tony called. “I have a question for you.”

“Oh, now you’re ready to talk?”

Tony got down on one knee and took his hand out of his pocket. He held an engagement ring.

“What’s this? You can’t. How did you?”

“May I ask my question now?”

BELIEF

"You're looking pretty smug."

"Well, shouldn't I?" Tony responded as he offered a wide grin. He was leaning back in his chair, looking up in the air, and letting the warm summer sun shine down on his face.

"I don't know," Kyle said. "Just because you're getting married to the prettiest girl in town doesn't give you the right to puff out your chest like that."

"It's offensive," Dave said. He was looking over the balcony at the river.

"I'll be sure to tone it back some for you both."

"But congrats, man. I'm excited for you."

"Thanks man. Cheers."

"OK. I've got to run." Kyle started to pat his pockets.

"Ha ha. Very funny."

"No, really. I think I forgot my wallet."

"I'll get this one. Again."

"You're so good to us, Dave!"

"Bite me."

Tony and Dave waved Kyle good-bye. The two sat in silence for some time, enjoying one of those perfect Friday evenings after work.

"You are looking different," Dave finally said, breaking the silence. "You look like you're back."

"Hmm." Tony thought about that statement for a moment and then said, "I don't know if I would say that's true. I don't feel that I'm back the way I was by any means. I just feel different. I feel like a weight is off of me, but I don't necessarily know what was weighing me down. And on a day like this, I'm not sure if I care."

"Cheers to that."

"But I feel better. About myself. About who I am. About the past. I feel like I learned a lot, and I'm thankful. It's like you said. Our thoughts can lead to feelings. If I look at past events as learning opportunities rather than something painful or bad, I have a better attitude about what happened. And that seems to be helping me in how I act today."

"Another cheers," Dave said as he tipped his glass slightly to Tony.

"You helped out so much, Dave. It really meant a lot. Thank you. But what happens if it happens again? I feel great now, but in just thinking about a meeting I have next week, I find myself feeling scared or nervous."

"It will happen again. You've had a great run lately. But know it'll happen again. You'll fail soon enough."

"Wow, thanks for the downer."

"I mean it. We all screw up. Remember, we're not striving for perfection. We can't have beautiful, perfect days like this one every day. When it does get cold or cloudy, remember that it's only a passing moment. Maybe it lasts longer than you want it to, but with what you've learned, you can be prepared for those moments. You need to go back to the process."

"I do feel like I'm better prepared for the next time."

"Absolutely. The experience you gained gives you the knowledge that you can come back again. Even if you forget everything that you've worked on, remember that you've overcome something. That's worth something for the next time it happens."

Tony raised his glass. "To next time?"

"To next time."

MAKING YOUR OWN MOVES

At some point in the past, someone or something may have ingrained a doubt or a feeling in you that continued to slowly build, like a snowball forming, throughout your life. Or perhaps these thoughts and feelings are new because of something that happened recently—something you did or think you did. Making a mistake, or failing, can send you down a similar path.

But whether you've been dealing with these feelings throughout your life or more recently, it's important to remember that these are habits that you've formed. You've reinforced them by repeating them over and over again. Now you have an opportunity to learn new behaviors. Just as you practiced these wrong feelings, you can rewire yourself to practice new and better ones. The following guide is meant to help you get out of your own head and develop a new way.

Challenge 1: Desire for Approval

As humans, we can be pretty hard on ourselves, even over the course of a normal day. We usually don't make it known to others, but our head trash can have a significant impact on our lives. Head trash, or the negative self-talk we say to ourselves, can influence our belief in ourselves. Simply thinking "I can't do this" when facing a new task can create a spiral of self-doubt and lack of action. Those thoughts of self-doubt lead to confirmed beliefs, which can lead to actions of perceived failure.

These actions of perceived failure are shown in simple day-to-day behaviors. We may not prepare for a presentation or an important meeting because we "didn't have time." Or we don't try new or different experiences because we don't believe we are good enough. Our body language sends a message of perceived failure through slumped shoulders, quiet voices, or our arms crossed over our chest. If we believe we can't do it, we'll prove ourselves right soon enough.

When we doubt ourselves over and over, we create an emotional void in our own self-belief. Over time, that void can grow larger as we continue to doubt, dread, or deceive. This defines how we feel about ourselves. Without a strong self-belief (mind-set), we tend to use head trash and negative self-talk to define who we are. If we lack self-belief, we look to other people or things for that belief. We allow others to define who we are—and who we are not.

Analysis

The problem with the above is obvious when we read it, but difficult to recognize in the moment. When we fail, these thoughts tend to intensify. It's important to stop and ask yourself three questions when you're in this spot or feeling unsure of yourself:

- **Where are my feelings (of self) coming from? Where do I get my approval from?** This question is helpful to understand how you are filling up your belief. When thinking of yourself or a task you have to complete, are your thoughts coming from the thoughts and opinions others have of you? Or are you providing your own positive and constructive feedback?
- **Is what I'm feeling real, or is it a belief I have?** In times of stress, people resort to a fight-flight-or-fret response. Most of us tend to focus on the latter. We fret and hold ourselves back. We focus on maintaining the status quo of the void. We don't believe we can do better, and we get stuck. Asking yourself if your beliefs are real can help identify your true feelings and emotions.
- **How am I showing up in my day?** Self-doubt creates fear, which interferes with your level of creativity and confidence. Not having confidence in yourself can impact how you show up to others. If others perceive you as lacking confidence, their opinions can reinforce your own lack of confidence, and your fear continues to spiral. Fear can also affect how you go about finding solutions to problems. It can impact your ability to be creative or to accomplish some of your fundamental tasks during the day.

Action

To face this challenge, you need to define your own sense of belief. You must train yourself to speak better on your own behalf. If you don't, you are in essence accepting that your head trash is true. At the same time, you have to ensure you aren't allowing others to provide your own belief and approval of who you are or who you are not. "You are what you say you are," says author Steven Pressfield in his book *The War of Art*. "You have to say it to be it." This can be easier said than done, but you can make changes with these simple tools and habits:

- **Take out your own head trash.** Replace the head trash and negative self-talk by creating a new voice. The next time you hear head trash, challenge the voice in your head. Confirm whether the words are trash or true. It's easy to recognize statements like "I'm not good at something." But what if the trash is "I really blew that project"? There might be some truth in there, but you're probably harder on yourself than others would be. Identify the negative talk and write down what you're saying to yourself. And then ask, is that true, or is it only your perception?
- **Respond to yourself like you would to others.** Would you tell someone they were a failure? I doubt it. Most of us are harder on ourselves than we are on others. It's important that you find ways to be kinder to yourself. As you look at the list of negative talk you wrote down, ask yourself if you would say each statement to a close friend, a family member, or a colleague. If not—and I hope not—write down what you would say to them. Use those words to reply to yourself every time head trash enters your mind.
- **Develop a plan for the worst-case scenario.** So many times with head trash we think of all the negative and awful things that could happen. "If I don't finish that project, I'll get fired." "If I say something at a meeting, everyone will laugh at me." Rather than ignore these feelings, try to visualize the worst-case scenario. Imagine the worst thing that could happen. When you visualize it, you realize that it is a pretty far-fetched scenario, and it allows you to know how to respond when it actually happens. In times of failure, we think we might get

fired or someone might yell at us. In reality, that person could be upset. But if you think through the worst-case scenario, you can also visualize what would really occur and how you could respond.

- **Treat negative feedback as feedback.** It hurts to hear negative feedback when it comes from someone you look up to. Even worse is when a friend or close co-worker says something that feels personal or hurtful when you're already feeling down. As difficult as it may be, take the time to find something you can take away from the comment and try differently next time. By learning from the feedback, you decrease the hurt feelings.
- **Visualize the process, not the outcome.** The best athletes in the world think through and visualize every aspect of an important competition. However, the rest of us do little to prepare for our day or an important meeting or event. Take time to visualize how things, even the small things, will unfold. If preparing for a meeting, for example, walk through how you'll open the door, how'll you'll greet others, what you'll say to start the meeting. If you're facing a difficult conversation, talk through how you'll respond to feedback that might be hard to hear. By visualizing each step, you focus on the actions that can lead to a successful outcome rather than the outcome itself.
- **Fake it until you make it.** When you doubt, you are less confident. Less courageous. Less creative. You may pass up opportunities to try new things. You tend to hide. When you fail, life does go on. If you aren't showing up confident, you will continue to drag yourself down with the head trash you say to yourself. If you are showing others you are not as confident, you may give the impression that you are not

engaged. When you get to this stage, you may have to push yourself to do something you don't want to do. For example, you may have to say something positive about yourself. Or lead a meeting after you've made a mistake. Remember, you don't have to like doing it; you just have to do it.

- **Pay attention to your body language.** Our bodies give us away. Slumped shoulders, folded arms, and gazes pointed down show you're closed down. Focus on opening yourself up. Practicing simple poses before starting your day or going into a difficult discussion can help you open up and appear more confident. The first pose is to reach your arms up, as if you are making a V. The second is to stick your chest out like Superman. Hold each of these poses for at least 20 seconds, or if you're feeling good, up to a minute. Not only will these poses help your posture show others that you're confident, but you'll feel confident as well.

Challenge 2: Giving up Control

When we lack a strong sense of belief, it can seem that we hand over the keys to our lives. We give up control. As we do this, other things dictate what is important to us, what we should spend our time on, and what we believe, or don't believe, in ourselves.

This can happen slowly over time, without us even recognizing it. Perhaps we stop doing the hobbies we used to enjoy. We may pull away from close friends or family members. Or we increase the number of hours we work, but we don't increase the value or productivity with those extra hours. We make excuses for why these things happen. We talk about how busy we are. That we have to get our work done "or else." But what we're really saying is that something is now more important than what truly matters to us.

Although it would be easy to blame others for this lack of control, at the end of the day, we are the only one in the driver's seat. It falls on us to decide whether to make a change or to remain in the passenger seat of our own life. Life is like money. It's up to you in how you want to spend it. To make positive steps forward, you have to take back control of your life.

When we fail, we tend to go to two extremes. First, we take on too much—too much work or too many activities that add little or no value to us or our employer. Second, we lose ownership of our actions. "It's not my fault I'm so busy; just look at everything that has to be done around here!"

Only by taking full ownership, focusing on what is most important and what we can control, can we learn from the failure and take action toward real change.

Analysis

This exchange of control occurs more frequently as we're falling after failure. After we've failed, or believe we've failed, we don't believe we have the right to continue to control our lives. We think that because of the mistake, we somehow aren't good enough anymore. Once we believe that, we slowly shut down. We stop doing the things that matter to us. We take this punishment we've given ourselves and wait for more because we believe we deserve it. We don't believe we deserve better. During these times, it's important to ask:

- **What are my priorities right now?** When you give up control of your life, you may not be spending your time on the right things. You may not be focused on work or on the hobbies and activities you love. Or you may be overly focused, forgetting about other relationships in your life.

- **What is the outcome that matters most within each priority?** When your priorities are off, so are your beliefs and behaviors. You may have changed some of the behaviors that made you successful. Or you've created new, undesirable behaviors. You must understand what you're focused on. Is it on the outcome? On something that is out of your control? Or are you focused on the behaviors that you can control and that you desire to create the outcome?
- **What do I need to take responsibility for?** If you lose focus on what matters to you, you may take on what matters to others. You start living another life, comparing yourself to others, and attaching yourself to outcomes or avoiding responsibility for your actions.

Action

To reclaim control, you have to focus on yourself, not the failure. Only you can improve your health, your career, and your social connections. Does that sound selfish? Perhaps, but if you think about it, who else is thinking about you? Think about the safety procedures you hear onboard an airplane before the flight takes off. If there is a decrease in cabin pressure, masks will drop from the ceiling to provide oxygen for the passengers. The flight attendants tell you that if you're traveling with someone who would need help with their mask, you should put your mask on first and then assist the other person. It's similar at work and in your life. Others rely on you to get the job done. But in order to help, you need to make sure you are physically and mentally at your best to do your job. The following advice can ensure you're able to do that:

- **Care for your entire well-being.** Are you focusing on the right things in your life? Do you know the right things to focus on? To have a strong well-being, you have to make time for the following areas:

- **Physical.** This is how you take care of your body. How you move, sleep, and eat. Adding positive habits around how you treat your body is critical to ensuring you're able to perform at your best every day.
- **Mindfulness.** Mindfulness is the act of focusing our attention on the present moment. We are aware of our emotions and able to acknowledge those emotions, as well as ourselves, without judgment. What you say and do in your mind is as important as, or more important than, your physical health. You need to ensure your mind, and your mind-set, is as healthy as the rest of your body. You can achieve this through meditation. Or try simpler activities such as setting aside some time at the beginning or end of the day to have a moment of gratitude. Remembering all of the things you are grateful for can help in your efforts toward better control and empathy.
- **Relationships.** The health of your relationships and your connections to others are also important to your well-being. Think about the connections that are most meaningful to you. Also think about the people whom you need to continue to build relationships with or, in some cases, rebuild relationships with.
- **Purpose.** Purpose comes from the activities that provide a sense of meaning for you. This can include the above areas; many people find meaning in their relationships with others or by exercising regularly. However, careers create a significant sense of purpose for people. When you like what you do and find meaning in what you do, you derive a strong sense of well-being from your career.

Because careers can contribute significantly to purpose, many people put a great deal of emphasis on this part of their lives. However, if you go too far, you run the risk of harming your overall well-being and your relationships with those close to you. You may work long hours, which limits the time you can spend with friends and family. You may say you're too busy to take care of your body or mind. Or you may not have the energy to pursue the other things in your life that give you a sense of purpose. Take a look at your life and make sure the areas that give you a sense of purpose are balanced.

- **"I will" set goals.** Although you may know what is important to you and what you need to focus on, it can be difficult to stay on track. You get distracted, you lose focus, you get in your own way. When you set goals, you create a constant reminder of what's important to you. Goals can be your road map in achieving a better sense of control. Start by creating one "I will" statement for each of the above categories, and set the deadline for completing it in 90 days, or a quarter of the year. These "I will" statements become the mission statement to help you achieve your goal. Saying the "I will" statement to yourself reminds you about what is important. Saying "I will" to others is more powerful than "I'd like" or "I hope to." Speaking those two words out loud to others helps hold you accountable. By creating "I will" statements quarterly instead of annually, you establish a habit that will help you create more achievable goals for a more successful outcome.
- **Prioritize the priorities.** Author Greg McKeown says in his book *Essentialism: The Disciplined Pursuit of Less*, "If you don't prioritize your life, someone else will." When you fail,

you start saying yes to everything because you believe that is what you have to do. You don't believe you have the option to say no to something because you believe you need to make up for your mistake or you aren't good enough to stand up for yourself. The reality is that by saying yes to everything, by constantly being busy, you give up control of your life. You give the impression that your time isn't valuable, that you aren't valuable. You have to continue to show your value, not by making up for a mistake you made, but by focusing on what is important to you.

Challenge 3: Lack of Empathy

The final challenge is a lack of empathy. At its most basic definition, empathy is the ability to understand and share the feelings of others. As we fail, we close down and stop being vulnerable to others. In the process, we lose our ability to empathize with others, to understand and show compassion to those around us. These actions can have disastrous results in our close relationships. If we're not vulnerable to close family and friends, we can alienate them. As leaders at work, our moods and behaviors can have a similar result. By shutting down to our colleagues, we cause our own performance and our team's performance to suffer.

But before we can be vulnerable with others, we have to be vulnerable within. We must empathize with ourselves. Before we stand in someone else's shoes, we must know what it's like to stand in our own shoes.

However, if we've failed, we've likely lost approval and given up control already. If we've failed, we don't forgive ourselves because we don't believe we should forgive ourselves. Furthermore, we've also lost the understanding of and compassion for who we are, what our strengths are, and what makes us who we are.

To truly climb back up and move forward, we must be able to forgive—our faults, our failures, and the weaknesses we believe we have. We have to acknowledge who we are and that all of those things combined—our strengths and weaknesses—make up who we are. We have to empathize with ourselves.

Without knowing how to empathize with ourselves, we're unable to empathize with others, to understand their strengths and weaknesses. And realize that they, too, are human.

Analysis

Having a lack of empathy is the most critical challenge. As we fall after failure, this lack of understanding can cause us to spiral into a deeper sense of inaccurate self-belief. We continue to doubt ourselves. We accumulate more and more head trash. We believe we've hit rock bottom because we've allowed ourselves to. That we deserve to be there.

But if we can empathize with ourselves, we can move forward. If we can find compassion for ourselves, we can begin to build ourselves back up.

- **What am I hanging on to?** We are all hanging on to something from the past. If you've failed, you need to go back to the scene of the crime. As much as you may want to forget it ever happened, you need to investigate. You need to truly understand the details of the event, how you got there, and how you, and others, were affected during and after.
- **How is this affecting how I view others?** After we fail, we tend to close down and stop being vulnerable to others. Some people may go into hiding; they avoid others for fear that they don't belong anymore or have lost their trust. Other people may respond by pointing fingers or reacting in anger.

You need to understand how you view others and how this affects your relationships.

- **How does this affect how I view myself?** Empathy is often thought of as a way to understand what it's like to stand in someone else's shoes. However, before you stand in someone else's shoes, you must know what it's like to stand in your own shoes. When you fail, it's important to understand how you are viewing yourself. If you are unable to understand and find compassion for yourself, your ability to regain control and find approval will be extremely difficult, perhaps almost impossible.

Action

It may seem difficult to find compassion for yourself when you are at your lowest. But without this fundamental practice, you will be unable to pick yourself back up and regain approval and control of yourself. Self-awareness is critical in order to create a level of compassion so you can forgive yourself and others.

There is an interesting phenomenon that happens when we fail. We tend to dwell on it, thinking of nothing but the failure. However, we also want to forget the failure ever happened. Unfortunately, neither action helps us move forward. In fact, dwelling on the mistake or ignoring it altogether increases the likelihood that we will fall deeper into giving up control and approval. To truly move on, we must fight the urge to hastily move on from the failure and instead:

- **Honestly review.** Put yourself back in your shoes and review the event not from a view of judgment, but from one of compassion. When you've failed, it's difficult to see what came out of the event other than the failure itself. However, you miss the value that can be learned, the positive things you may have done, and what you need to avoid in the future. So make a list of the specific things that happened at that event. Start with the easier items, such as how you talk about the situation to yourself or others. But then ask "why?" or "what else?" to capture everything that came out of the event. Write down everything that comes to mind.

- **Acknowledge the lessons.** For each item, ask yourself what you could have done differently. Write down your ideas. What do you need to do to improve next time? At the same time, acknowledge those things that went well. Reviewing the event with an eye toward learning can help you move forward without carrying the failure as baggage.
- **Share with others.** As you learn to empathize with yourself, you will have to take an honest look from within. Once you've acknowledged what you've learned, you will want to consider talking openly with those who were involved. If it's your boss, you probably think you've talked too much about the failure! However, this isn't a time to dredge up old details, but to confirm what you've learned. As you share your lessons, ask for the other person's thoughts and if they saw anything else that you can learn from. When it's time to share with your team, approach the discussion with the same eye toward learning. This isn't a time for judgment, but an opportunity to continue to find ways to improve. As you reach out to others, you must believe they are trying to help. Although you may get feedback that could be difficult to hear, keep in mind that those around you want you to get better; this will help you take in what they have to say.
- **Be grateful.** If you approach the failure as an opportunity to truly learn, then you can be grateful for the learning that you receive. You can forgive yourself and others who

were involved. You're not letting yourself off the hook, but allowing yourself the opportunity to learn from the event and apply those lessons to future situations. If you can learn from the event, then there is nothing left to hang on to. Periodically, review what you wrote down and consider how you've applied those lessons. This isn't dwelling, but allowing yourself to look at what you've been able to change because of your learning.

As you analyze your feelings and implement the action steps in each of the three areas (desire for approval, giving up control, and lack of empathy), give yourself time. You won't reverse your negative thinking, feelings, and behaviors overnight. Don't get discouraged if you see yourself making progress, but then find that you've taken a step or two back. That's natural. As you keep working at these areas, you'll find that, over time, you have a better perspective on old failures and you're responding to new failures in a healthier way. These reactions are signs that you're developing belief in yourself and are no longer seeking the approval of others, giving up control, or lacking empathy. These are essential steps in becoming the leader, and person, you want to be.

ABOUT THE AUTHOR

photo credit Chandra Ostrognai

Mike Bensi writes and teaches on creating strategies to help organizations transform their cultures, employees, and the leaders who support them.Throughout his career, first as a manager and now as a consultant, he has worked with hundreds of senior leaders, as well as new supervisors and managers, throughout various industries. He holds an MBA from the Indiana University Kelley School of Business. Mike lives in the Indianapolis, IN area with his wife and three children.

CPSIA information can be obtained
at www.ICGtesting.com
Printed in the USA
LVHW111402070220
646217LV00001B/91

9 781683 504245